GOVERNING AND TEACHING

A SOURCEBOOK ON COLONIAL AMERICA

GOVERNING AND TEACHING

A SOURCEBOOK ON COLONIAL AMERICA

Edited by Carter Smith

AMERICAN ALBUMS FROM THE COLLECTIONS OF
THE LIBRARY OF CONGRESS

THE MILLBROOK PRESS, *Brookfield, Connecticut*

Cover: *A view of the Statehouse in Philadelphia in 1799, printed by William Birch.*

Title Page: *An etching of the city of Philadelphia, eastern view, 1768.*

Contents Page: *Seal of the Council for New England.*

Back Cover: *"The Bloody Massacre Perpetrated in King Street, Boston, on March 5th, 1770, by a Part of the 29th Regiment." Engraving (hand-colored) by Paul Revere.*

Library of Congress Cataloging-in-Publication Data

Governing and Teaching: a sourcebook on colonial America / edited by
Carter Smith.
     p. cm. -- (American albums from the collections of the Library of
Congress)
     Includes bibliograpical references and index.
     Summary: Describes and illustrates the historical, political, and
religious aspects of life in colonial America through a variety of images
produced during that time.
     ISBN 1-56294-036-8
     1. United States--Civilization--To 1783--Juvenile literature. 2. United
States--Civilization--To 1783--Sources--Juvenile literature. 3. United
States--Politics and government--Colonial period, ca. 1600-1775-
Juvenile literature. 4. United States--Politics and government--Colonial
period, ca. 1600-1775--Sources--Juvenile literature. 5. United States--
Politics and government--Revolution, 1775-1783--Juvenile literature. 6.
United States--Politics and government--Revolution, 1775-1783--
Sources--Juvenile literature. [1. United States--History--Colonial period,
ca. 1600-1775--Sources. 2. United States--Politics and government--
Colonial period, ca. 1600-1775--Sources.] I. Smith, C. Carter. II. Series.
E162.G68 1991
973.2--dc20
                                                              91-13937
                                                                  CIP
                                                                   AC

 Created in association with Media Projects Incorporated

C. Carter Smith, *Executive Editor*
Lelia Wardwell, *Managing Editor*
Charles A. Wills, *Consulting Editor*
Kimberly Horstman, *Researcher*
Lydia Link, *Designer*
Athena Angelos, *Photo Researcher*

The consultation of Bernard F. Reilly, Jr., Head Curator of the
Prints and Photographs Division of the Library of Congress, is
gratefully acknowledged.

10 9 8 7 6 5 4 3 2 1

Contents

Introduction   7

Part I: 1490-1649
The First Settlers   11

Part II: 1650-1754
Change and Conflict   33

Part III: 1755-1775
The Way to Independence   61

Resource Guide   94

Index   95

COGNITA MIHI

GENS IN SERVIET

William Brewster (1567-1644) was one of the leaders of the Pilgrims, who broke away from the Church of England in 1606. He joined the Plymouth Colony, which was set up in Massachusetts by the Pilgrims who arrived on the Mayflower *in 1620. As a church elder, Brewster was a religious leader for the colony, conducting services of prayer and praise for his congregation.*

Introduction

GOVERNING AND TEACHING is one of the volumes in a series of books that are titled AMERICAN ALBUMS FROM THE COLLECTIONS OF THE LIBRARY OF CONGRESS. The first six books in the series are subtitled SOURCEBOOKS ON COLONIAL AMERICA. They treat the early history of our homeland from its discovery and early settlement through the colonial and Revolutionary wars.

The editor's basic goal for the series is to make available to the student many of the original visual documents—the early maps, prints, drawings, engravings, and broadsides—preserved in the Library of Congress as records of the American past. An attempt has been made to rely as heavily as possible on works contemporaneous with the events and people portrayed. This affords the student contact with the primary materials used by historians, and provides a window on the colonial world. Some later images, either creative reconstructions of earlier events or renderings of historical sites as they survived in the nineteenth century, provide a look back at the colonial period from a closer vantage point. In some cases these later works present a more heroic, Eurocentric picture of American history than that to which we would subscribe today, but in most cases the images provide the only authentic records of the now-vanished buildings and towns of early America.

Each of these visual sourcebooks also includes, in addition to the images, several illustrated timelines, which provide a chronology of the main political, military, and cultural events of the period.

GOVERNING AND TEACHING reproduces original prints, maps, and book illustrations preserved in the special collections divisions of the Library of Congress, and a few from its general book collections. Many of the images in this volume come from contemporary accounts of early voyages and settlements which are housed in the Library's Rare Book and Special Collections Division.

Many of the works reproduced in this album are among the earliest surviving eyewitness portrayals of the New World. These prints and maps were part of the great mass of new intelligence about the West Indies which poured into Europe during the era of exploration. The engravings of the native inhabitants of Virginia encountered by the early British colonists, which appeared in Thomas Hariot's *A Briefe and True Report of the New Found Land of Virginia*, copy the watercolor drawings of John White, an artist sent by Walter Raleigh to help found that British colony.

Other of the maps and plates appearing here were based upon written accounts rather than first-hand knowledge, and are at times colored by the views and biases of their publishers. As a result some are less than truthful. Other writers and their illustrators accented the savagery of the Indians in a way consistent with existing European notions of primitive cultures.

In contrast to the exploration literature, there are few contemporaneous images of life in Puritan New England. The art of engraving or picture-making was a luxury trade. What does exist are the portraits of Protestant religious leaders such as George Whitefield and Jonathan Edwards, which accompanied books of their writings or lives. In addition, there were several engravings of the great institutions and schools, such as Harvard and Yale, produced to display the progress of civilization in the colonies. For other aspects of life in this period, we turn to nineteenth-century portrayals produced by the first generation of American illustrators, such as F. O. C. Darley and Benson Lossing. These citizens of a country just old enough to have a proper history began to reconstruct, in their art, the American past.

The pictorial documents included here represent a small but telling portion of the rich record of the American past that the Library of Congress preserves in its role as the national library.

BERNARD F. REILLY, JR.

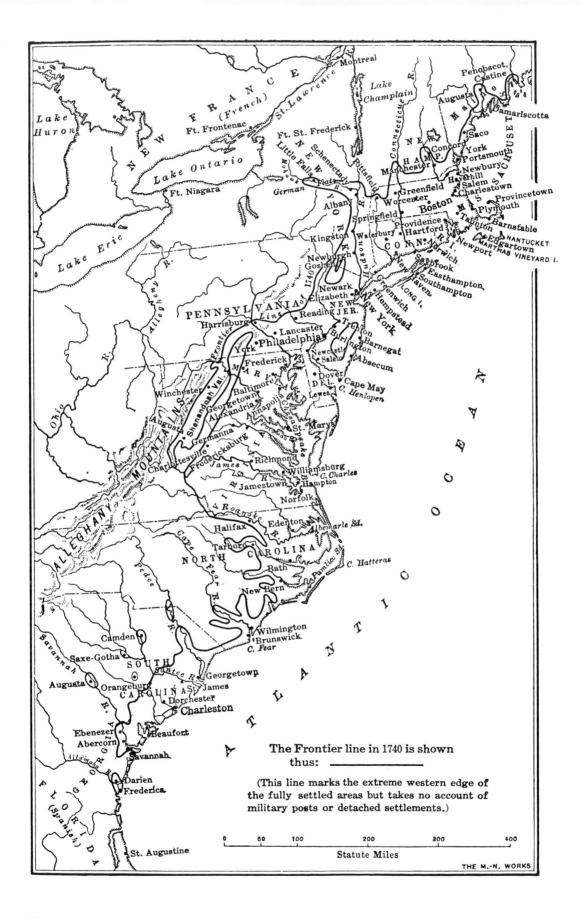

The Frontier line in 1740 is shown
thus: ———————

(This line marks the extreme western edge of
the fully settled areas but takes no account of
military posts or detached settlements.)

| 0 | 50 | 100 | 200 | 300 | 400 |

Statute Miles

THE M.-N. WORKS

The Colonies in 1700

By 1700, North America was divided into two great colonial empires—New France and the English colonies. Spain, the first European power in the New World, still controlled what would become the southwestern United States. By the end of the seventeenth century Spanish influence east of the Mississippi River was limited to Florida.

New France, while far smaller than the English colonies in population, was a vast land. To the north and east, France was well-established in the St. Lawrence River valley and on the islands at the river's mouth. To the west, France controlled the enormous wilderness between the Mississippi River and the Allegheny mountains. While rich in furs, this territory was home to only scattered settlements and missions, mostly along the Mississippi and Ohio rivers.

While France controlled the interior, England maintained a string of colonies along the Atlantic coast. In 1607, the Jamestown settlement was established in Virginia. Thirteen years later, the Pilgrims arrived in what would become New England. Puritans established the Massachusetts Bay Colony in 1629, followed by Connecticut (1639), Rhode Island (1644), and New Hampshire (1679). To the south, Maryland was founded—originally as a refuge for English Roman Catholics—in 1632, and settlers arrived in Carolina in 1670. (The colony was divided into North and South Carolina in the 1720s.)

By 1700, England had also gained the middle-Atlantic region, which had divided New England from the southern colonies. New Amsterdam became the city of New York in 1644, and in 1685 much of the rest of New Netherland became the colony of New York. East and West Jersey, united as New Jersey in 1702, were established in 1676. William Penn founded Pennsylvania in 1682, gaining the territory that became Delaware the next year. Thus, by 1700, twelve of the thirteen colonies that became the original United States had been settled.

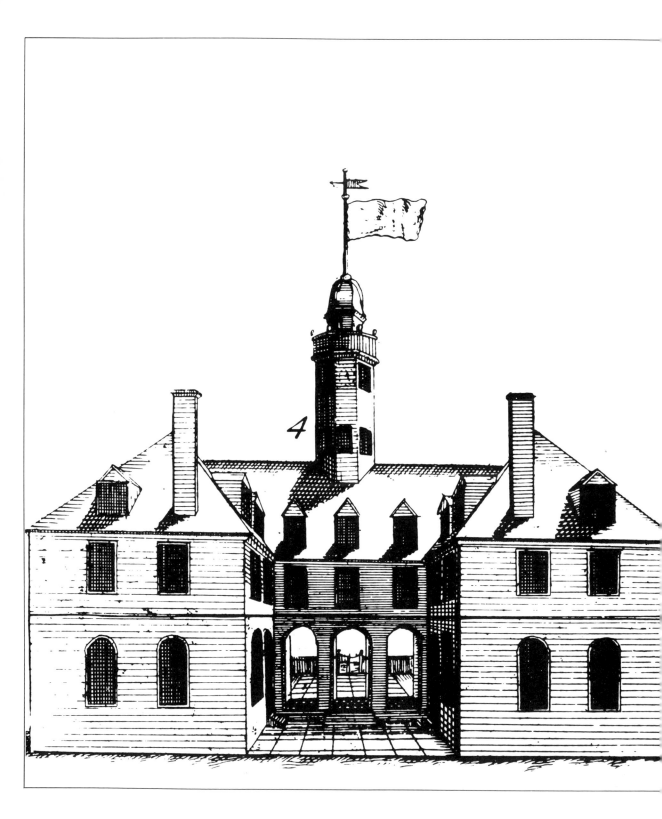

Part I: 1490-1649
The First Settlers

The first government council in North America was the House of Burgesses in Jamestown, Virginia. The members met for the first time in the summer of 1619. The House of Burgesses moved to the town of Williamsburg, Virginia, in 1669. This drawing of the Williamsburg meeting house originally came from the Bodleian Library in Oxford.

Of all the European nations, Spain was in the best position to begin colonizing the New World. Spain was a united and secure nation in the sixteenth century, unlike France and England. Christopher Columbus discovered America on a voyage sponsored by the Spanish crown. After Columbus's journey, more and more Spanish explorers came to the New World seeking riches. They seized territories from the Indians and claimed them for Spain. In the course of their conquests, the Spanish sought to convert the Indians to Christianity, as a way to show Spanish support for the Catholic Church.

One of the greatest changes to take place in Europe in the sixteenth century was the Reformation. This religious revolution challenged the teachings and practices of the Roman Catholic Church. The followers of this new branch of Christianity, called Protestants, refused to recognize the Pope as the head of the Christian Church. Many Protestants suffered cruel persecution for their beliefs. They began coming to the New World toward the end of the sixteenth century to escape this harsh treatment and to set up colonies of their own where they could live and worship in peace.

Desire for wealth was another reason colonies were founded in the New World. Merchants, particularly in England, formed companies that sponsored expeditions to America.

The first European settlers had to struggle to survive in the new lands. They found strength and comfort in their religion, which brought both unity and education to the settlements.

A TIMELINE OF MAJOR EVENTS

PART I *1490-1649 The First Settlers*

1490-1549

WORLD HISTORY

Columbus sets out for America

1492 Spain is finally united under Ferdinand and Isabella; the nation is now able to devote attention to exploration. Christopher Columbus claims North America for Spain.

1510 Portugal founds the first European colony in India, at Goa.

1517 German monk Martin Luther protests abuses in the Roman Catholic Church, beginning the Protestant Reformation.

1519 Charles I of Spain becomes ruler of the Holy Roman Empire, which includes much of central Europe.

1520 Sulayman I, "The Magnificent," becomes sultan of Turkey; Turkey's empire now includes Arabia.

1526 The Mogul dynasty is established in India.

1534 The English Parliament passes the Act of Supremacy acknowledging Henry VIII as head of the Church of England, beginning the English Reformation.

1546 The Catholic Counter-Reformation begins in an attempt to reverse the gains made by Protestantism.

1547 Ivan IV, "The Terrible," is crowned czar of Russia.

COLONIAL HISTORY GOVERNMENT

1494 Pope Alexander VI issues the Treaty of Tordesillas, dividing the New World between Spain and Portugal.

1499 Spanish settlers on the island of Hispaniola (today the nations of Haiti and the Dominican Republic) revolt against Columbus's government of the colony.

1500 Columbus, accused of mismanagement and cruelty by the Hispaniola colonists, is returned to Spain in chains.

1501 King Ferdinand of Spain institutes laws to govern Spain's growing New World colonies.

1512 Spain issues the Laws of Burgos, which are designed to protect Indians from cruel

Pope Alexander VI

treatment in Spain's colonies.

1518 Charles V, King of Spain and the Holy Roman Emperor, allows African slaves to be sent to the New World.

1532 To strengthen its colonies, the Spanish government requires ships sailing to the New World to carry livestock and seeds for crops.

1542 The Spanish government ends the practice of *encomienda*, a system that allowed colonists to tax New World Indians or force them to work.

COLONIAL HISTORY RELIGION AND EDUCATION

1508 Pope Julius II gives Spain the right to appoint Church officials for the New World.

1514 Spain institutes the *Requerimiento,* a law requiring all Indians in Spain's New World possessions to convert to Christianity or face slavery or death.

1517 Bartolomé de Las Casas, a Spanish priest, urges better treatment

Bartolomé de Las Casas

of the native population in Spain's New World possessions; Las Casas is also the first Roman Catholic priest ordained in the New World.

1538 Spain establishes the first university in the New World on the Caribbean island of Santo Domingo.

1540 Four Franciscan friars accompany Coronado's expedition through southwestern North America.

1544 Spanish friar Juan de Padilla is killed by Indians in what is now New Mexico, becoming the first missionary to die in what will become the United States.

Coronado's expedition

1554 Queen Mary of England restores that nation to Catholicism.

1557 Portugal founds the colony of Macao on the Chinese coast.

1559 Elizabeth I becomes Queen of England, making the nation Protestant again.

1562 The Wars of Religion between French Catholics and French Protestants begin.

1566 Protestants in the Netherlands, then governed by Spain, revolt against Catholic rule.

1588 The Spanish Armada sails from Spain hoping to invade and conquer England; the Spanish fleet is destroyed by a combination of English warships and storms.

1594 Prince Henry of Navarre becomes King Henry IV of France.

1595 The Dutch East India Company sends trading expeditions to Asia.

1598 Henry IV proclaims the Edict of Nantes, granting equal rights to French Protestants and Catholics and ending the Wars of Religion.

1610 Henry IV of France is assassinated.

1618 The Thirty Years War begins; originally between Protestants

A German mercenary in the Thirty Years War

and Catholics in central Europe, the conflict becomes complicated as most of Europe joins in.

Totem of the five nations of the Iroquois Confederacy

1570 Five Indian tribes in northeastern North America join together to form the Iroquois Confederacy.

1583 Sir Humphrey Gilbert is granted a patent to colonize North America by Elizabeth, the Queen of England.

1595 Spain divides its territory in southwestern North America into missions governed by the Roman Catholic Church; the government hopes that conversion of Indians to Christianity, rather than military rule, will control the region.

1606 James I of England charters two companies, the Plymouth Company and the Virginia Company, to settle colonies in North America.

1607 The Jamestown Colony is founded; the settlement is governed by a council under the supervision of the Virginia Company in England.

1610 After nearly being abandoned, Jamestown

Seal of Virginia Company

is placed under virtual martial law by its new leader, Lord de la Warr.

1611 "Dale's Laws," a harsh series of rules governing the Jamestown Colony, go into effect.

1551 The first university in North America is established in Mexico City.

A Jesuit missionary

1570 Spanish Jesuit missionaries arrive in the Chesapeake Bay area; all are wiped out in Indian attacks within a year.

1571 The Inquisition, an organization devoted to rooting out "enemies" of the Roman Catholic Church, begins operating in Mexico; several Protestants are executed in the 1570s.

1595 Missionaries in Spanish Florida convert

more than a thousand Indians to Catholicism.

1605 An English expedition sails to North America hoping to find a place for English Roman Catholics to settle; no colony is founded, but the expedition sparks English interest in New World colonization.

1607 Among the first settlers at Jamestown is Robert Hunt, a Church of England minister.

Ruins of Jamestown's Church

1615 Four Franciscan friars arrive at Quebec, beginning French missionary efforts in New France.

A TIMELINE OF MAJOR EVENTS

PART I *1490-1649* *The First Settlers*

1619 - 1639

WORLD HISTORY

The Mayflower

1620 On September 6, a company of forty-six Pilgrims sailed from Southampton, England, for America.

King Charles I

1625 James I of England dies and is succeeded by Charles I.

1630 Gustavus Adolphus, King of Sweden, invades the Holy Roman Empire; he is killed in battle two years later.

1630-42 Some 16,000 colonists from England emigrate to Massachusetts.

1633 France declares war on Spain.

1637 Russian explorers reach the Pacific Ocean having crossed Siberia.

Gustavus Adolphus

1639 Through a series of decrees Japan is closed to foreigners.

COLONIAL HISTORY GOVERNMENT

1619 The first elected assembly in English North America—the Virginia House of Burgesses—holds its first session at Jamestown.

1620 The Pilgrims sign the Mayflower Compact while still aboard the Mayflower, binding the signers to obey "just and equal laws."

1623 "According to the commendable custom of England," the Pilgrims establish trial by twelve-man jury at Plymouth.

1627 The Company of New France, better known as "the Hundred Associates," gains control of France's North American colonies.

1630 John Billington of Plymouth becomes the first English colonist in North America to be hanged for murder.

1633 To reduce its dependence on tobacco, Virginia passes laws designed to diversify the colony's crops. The Puritan settlement at Dorchester in the Massachusetts Bay Colony organizes as a township, setting the pattern for local government in New England.

1635 A Maryland Indian leader protests the colony's insistence that Indians obey English law; instead, he suggests the colonists "conform to the customs of our country."

1636 Plymouth establishes representative government; previously, the colony had been governed by a "general court."

1639 Puritan towns in Connecticut unite under the Fundamental Orders, which declare

---

COLONIAL HISTORY RELIGION AND EDUCATION

1621 The Pilgrims at Plymouth hold a prayer service to dedicate the colony's Common House, which serves as both a church and a public meeting place.

1628 The first Dutch Reformed Church congregation is established in New Amsterdam.

1632 The Calverts, a prominent English Roman Catholic family,

are granted land for a colony in the northern part of Virginia.

1634 The Calverts establish Maryland as a refuge for English Roman Catholics.

1635 Roger Williams is banished from the Massachusetts Bay Colony for his unorthodox religious and political beliefs, which will later become the basis

for the Baptist Church.
•The Boston Latin School (still in existence) is founded.

1636 Roger Williams and his followers found Providence Plantations on Narragansett Bay; the colony is based on the concept of religious tolerance.
•Harvard College is founded.

1638 Swedish and Finnish settlers found New Sweden on the

Delaware, bringing Lutheranism to America.

Roger Williams flees Massachusetts

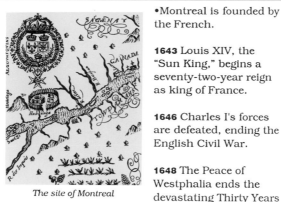

1640 Fredrick William succeeds his father, George William, as elector of Brandenburg.

1641 Catholics revolt in Ireland, some 30,000 Protestants are killed.

1642 The English Civil War begins: a conflict between supporters of Charles I and the Church of England and the largely Puritan supporters of Parliamentary government led by Oliver Cromwell. Many

The site of Montreal

supporters of the late King emigrate to America.

•Montreal is founded by the French.

1643 Louis XIV, the "Sun King," begins a seventy-two-year reign as king of France.

1646 Charles I's forces are defeated, ending the English Civil War.

1648 The Peace of Westphalia ends the devastating Thirty Years War. The Dutch and Swedish republics gain independence.

Oliver Cromwell

---

that "the foundation of authority is the free consent of the people."

1643 The Confederation of New England is founded to settle disputes and strengthen defenses against Indians and colonists of other nations.

1646 Virginia's Governor William Berkeley captures Chief Opechancanough, whose tribe had slaughtered 500 colonists in 1644.

Opechancanough and Captain John Smith

1647 Peter Stuyvesant, governor of New Netherland, jails

Peter Stuyvesant

Adriaen van der Donck; Stuyvesant hopes to stifle a growing movement for self-government in the Dutch colony.

1647 The Rhode Island colony adapts a liberal constitution.

1648 Margaret Brant, a wealthy Maryland landowner, asks for the right to vote in the colony's assembly; her request is denied. Massachusetts adopts the Cambridge Platform, which asserts the right of the Puritan Congregational Church to regulate behavior and civil government.

1642 The Massachusetts Bay Colony requires parents to make sure children can "read and understand the principles of Religion and the capitall lawes of the country."

1644 Roger Williams writes *The Bloudy Tenent of Persecution*; the book defends religious freedom and protests the Puritan attempt to unite all New England colonists into a single church.

•The General Court of Massachusetts orders all clergy to learn Indian dialects to aid religious conversions of the Indians.

1646 John Eliot, Puritan "Apostle to the Indians," begins missionary work among the Indians of New England.

1647 Massachusetts requires all towns with fifty families or more, to hire a teacher and provide public education.

1647 The first public school is established in Virginia by Benjamin Syms; a decade later it merges with the Eaton School to form the Syms-Eaton School, which still operates.

1649 Maryland's legislature passes the Tolerance Act, guaranteeing freedom of worship to most Christian churches.
•The Society for the Propagation of the Gospel is founded

in England; among its goals is missionary work among the Indians.
•Jean de Brébeouf, a Jesuit missionary in New France, is tortured to death by Iroquois Indians; in 1930, he is made a saint by the Roman Catholic Church.

CHRISTOPHER COLUMBUS

King Ferdinand and Queen Isabella of Spain, who sponsored Columbus's expedition, were not expecting to find new lands. Instead, they hoped Columbus would discover a new route to the capitals of Asia so they could participate in the silk and spice trade more easily. At that time, the only way to get to the East from Europe was by land, which was a long and costly journey. When Christopher Columbus arrived in the New World in 1492, he took the first step in bringing European systems of religion, government, and education to the Western Hemisphere. He returned to Spain and told Ferdinand and Isabella of his voyage. They immediately made him governor general of all lands he had discovered or would discover. He went back to the New World and founded a colony on the island of Hispaniola, in the Caribbean sea. Columbus showed greater skills as an explorer than as a governor, and he neglected his colony in order to search for new territories. When he returned to find Hispaniola in disorder, he ruled the colonists so strictly that many of them went back to Spain and complained. Columbus fell out of favor with the Spanish king as reports of the colony's miserable conditions spread. In 1500, Ferdinand and Isabella sent a new governor to Hispaniola to replace Columbus, who was sent back to Spain in chains.

P B Bouttats f

Christopher Columbus (1451-1506) departed from Palos, Spain, on August 3, 1492. In this illustration (left), he bids farewell to Ferdinand and Isabella. In the background, his men are boarding the expedition's three ships, the Niña, the Pinta, and the Santa Maria.

Columbus landed on one of the Bahama islands on October 12, 1492. He went on to discover other islands in the Caribbean, which he continued to believe were part of the East Indies. For this reason, he called the native people he met there "Indians." They are greeting Columbus with gifts of welcome in this engraving (below) by Theodore de Bry.

THE INDIANS, THE SPANISH AND THE ROMAN CATHOLIC CHURCH

Following the death of Columbus in 1506, more and more Spanish explorers set out across the Atlantic Ocean to discover and claim new territories for Spain. In the course of their expeditions, these *conquistadores* (which means "conquerors" in Spanish) encountered Native Americans whom they tried to convert to Roman Catholicism, often by force. Some Indians, when they set eyes on these enormous ships and white men in strange costumes, believed that the explorers were gods. The Spanish thought of the Indians as inferiors, "savages." The *conquistadores* enslaved the Indians and used forceful religious conversion as one way to keep the Indians under their control. Any Indian who resisted faced torture or death. Some religious leaders who accompanied these expeditions were more sympathetic to the Indians and set about establishing missions near Indian communities to teach them the ways of Christianity.

Bartolomé de Las Casas (1474-1566; opposite page, top) was a Catholic missionary who came to the Spanish island colony of Hispaniola in 1502. He spoke out against the cruel treatment of the Native Americans. In the 1540s, Las Casas helped draft the "New Laws." These were guidelines for the Spanish government designed to protect Indians in Spain's colonies from abuses.

Sometimes Indians were enlisted to help convert their own people to Christianity. Opechancanough was an Indian from Virginia who was picked up by a Spanish ship in 1561 and taken to Spain. There he was renamed Don Luis de Velasco and adopted by the Jesuits. The Jesuits, a Catholic religious order, taught him the language and culture of Spain. When Don Luis was returned to his people in 1570, he rejected his Jesuit tutors. In the end he killed them in a raid, shown in this drawing from a sixteenth-century book (opposite page, bottom), and destroyed the mission the Jesuits had established in Virginia.

Indian villages that resisted orders to convert to Christianity faced brutal attacks by the Spanish conquistadores. Without firearms, the Indians were usually the losers in these clashes, as illustrated (above) in an engraving by the Flemish artist Theodore de Bry.

THE FRENCH PROTESTANTS

The first Frenchmen to settle in the New World were part of a Protestant sect known in France as the *Huguenots*. Because of their religious beliefs, the Huguenots were often victims of discrimination and violence in France, and they wished to establish a colony of their own to escape this cruel treatment. An expedition of 150 men, led by Captain Jean Ribaut, reached what is now Florida in 1562. They established a settlement farther north in Port Royal, on Parris Island, North Carolina. Within a year, food and supplies ran so short that the surviving colonists abandoned their settlement and returned to France. A second group of Huguenots reached Florida in 1564, this time led by René de Laudonnière. The arrivals were greeted warmly by the Florida Indians, who had also welcomed Ribaut two years earlier. Under Laudonnière's leadership, Fort Caroline was built on the St. Johns River. The French colonists were threatened by the Spanish, who had settled nearby in St. Augustine. In 1565, Catholics and Protestants took up arms against each other in the New World. A Spanish force, led by Pedro Menéndez de Avilés, attacked Fort Caroline in October, and the French colonists were massacred.

When Jean Ribaut first arrived in Florida, he constructed a monument, bearing the arms of France, on the St. Johns River. When René de Laudonnière came in 1564, Athore, a Florida Indian chief, brought him and twenty of his men to see the monument (above), which the Indians were worshipping as a sacred idol.

This early map (right) of Florida was drawn in 1564 by Jacques Le Moyne de Morgues, a painter who accompanied Laudonnière on the second French expedition to Florida. The map shows only those places that the French had visited before establishing Fort Caroline. The coastline is inaccurate because the French had not explored the entire peninsula.

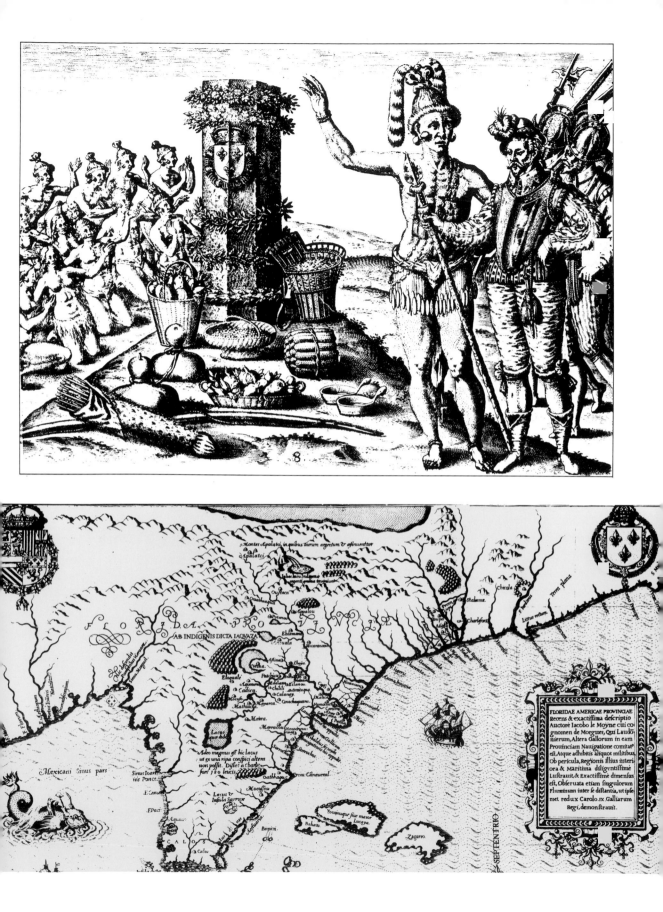

THE ROANOKE COLONY

Because of political and religious struggles in the first half of the sixteenth century, England was slow to plant colonies in the New World. When Elizabeth I came to the throne in 1558, England began to turn its attention to North America. After Sir Francis Drake sailed around the world in 1580, interest in the New World blossomed. The queen gave Sir Walter Raleigh, an adventurer who was a favorite of hers, a royal grant to explore, colonize, and govern new territories "not inhabited by Christian people." In 1584, Raleigh sent two English navigators, Philip Amadas and Arthur Barlowe, to North America. They returned to England with reports of the area along the coast of what is now North Carolina. Raleigh named the region "Virginia," after Queen Elizabeth, who was known as the Virgin Queen. Raleigh organized a colonizing expedition that landed on Roanoke Island in 1585. But Raleigh's attempts to establish a colony at Roanoke failed. The first expedition returned to England after a year, complaining of hardships and food shortages. Three years after a second settlement was established in 1587, all of the colonists had disappeared.

Sir Walter Raleigh (c. 1554-1618; above) never set foot in North America, although he sponsored two unsuccessful attempts to establish an English colony on Roanoke Island.

These engravings of an Indian chief and his wife (opposite page) are based on watercolors made by John White, an artist who led the first expedition to Roanoke the following year. White returned to England in 1586, bringing the first views of the Virginia Indians with him.

JAMESTOWN AND THE VIRGINIA INDIANS

England finally established a successful colony in the New World in 1607 through the efforts of the Virginia Company of London, a group of merchants. The settlement was named Jamestown after King James I of England. Living conditions in the colony were difficult, and the settlers, mostly soldiers or gentlemen, were not accustomed to hard labor. Many of the new arrivals had come in hopes of finding gold and had no interest in building shelters or planting crops. The council members who were supposed to govern the colony argued among themselves and accomplished little. Captain John Smith, one of the leaders of the group, helped restore order by forcing the colonists to work. Their efforts brought them into conflict with the local Indians, who saw the settlement as an invasion of their land. Smith was captured by the Indians in 1608. According to his own account, Smith would have been executed if the chief's daughter, Pocahontas, hadn't saved his life. Smith learned to speak the Indians' language and managed to set up friendly terms with them. The two groups lived together peacefully for several years after this incident.

Captain John Smith (1580-1631; above) joined the Virginia Company of London in 1606. He came along on the Jamestown expedition in 1607. Without his skillful leadership and his ability to deal with the Indians, the Jamestown colony probably would have failed.

This engraving (above), based on a painting by John White, shows the Virginia Indians engaged in a dance, at a gathering from several nearby villages. The English colonists at Jamestown did not understand Indian rituals, and often judged them as "savage," anti-Christian practices.

THE PILGRIMS AND THE MAYFLOWER COMPACT

The second permanent English colony in North America was established in Plymouth, Massachusetts, in 1620. The new arrivals, now known as the Separatists or Pilgrims, were a religious group that disagreed with the teachings and practices of the Church of England. They emigrated first to Holland, then set out aboard the *Mayflower* for Virginia. The Pilgrims landed at what is now Plymouth, Massachusetts, far north of Virginia. When they realized they would be settling outside of the Virginia Company's territory, they decided to organize their own government. Before leaving the ship, the Pilgrims drew up an agreement known as the Mayflower Compact. The compact was a simple agreement that the settlers would consult each other on all matters affecting the community, and make decisions by voting. The Mayflower Compact was an important step toward self-government in the colonies.

The Pilgrims gathered to sign the Mayflower Compact while the ship was still anchored in Plymouth harbor, as shown in this nineteenth-century illustration (right). Governor William Bradford (c.1590-1657) is shown in the center reading the agreement aloud to the others.

This map (above), dated 1634, shows the coastline of Massachusetts, where the Pilgrims landed in 1620. The landing party first came ashore at the tip of Cape Cod on November 11. They explored the coastline over the next several weeks and decided to build their colony farther north, on Plymouth harbor.

THE PURITANS: GOVERNING THROUGH THE CHURCH

Like the Pilgrims, the Puritans objected to the Church of England. But rather than separating from the English church, the Puritans hoped they could reform it from within. When Charles I, the son of James I, ascended the English throne in 1625, the Puritans worried that he would be hostile to their beliefs and practices. They formed their own company, the Massachusetts Bay Company, and received a charter from the king to establish a colony in North America. In 1630 they sent eleven ships, carrying more than seven hundred men, women, and children, to New England. The colonists settled in Massachusetts Bay, near what is now the city of Boston. The colony grew steadily, and by the 1640s, about 20,000 settlers had come to New England. John Winthrop, who led the original expedition, became the colony's elected governor, and ruled the Puritan settlement according to strict religious codes. Those colonists who did not follow these codes were often driven out of the settlement altogether. A minister named Roger Williams particularly angered the Puritan leaders by arguing that church and state should be kept apart. Williams was banished from Massachusetts in 1635. He established a settlement of his own, which he named Providence, in what is now Rhode Island.

John Winthrop (1588-1649; above) was a prominent member of the Massachusetts Bay Company who abandoned his law practice in London to lead the Puritan expedition to the New World. As governor of the community from 1630 to 1649, he did not tolerate individuals who expressed religious views different from those of the Puritans.

Roger Williams (c.1603-83) published this book (right) about Indian languages in 1643. The first phrase Williams translated and printed was "I love you." After Williams was expelled from Boston, he was befriended by the Narragansett Indians of Rhode Island. He purchased land from them and founded the town of Providence in 1636.

This drawing (below), by nineteenth-century artist Howard Pyle, shows a Puritan leader publicly scolding citizens for drinking and gambling in a village inn. Proper behavior was important to the Puritans, who wanted their community to be free from the "wordly" practices and customs they had left behind in England.

A KEY into the
LANGUAGE
OF
AMERICA:
OR,
An help to the *Language* of the *Natives* in that part of A M E R I C A, called *NEW-ENGLAND.*

Together, with briefe *Observations* of the Cuftomes, Manners and Worfhips, &c. of the aforefaid *Natives*, in Peace and Warre, in Life and Death.

On all which are added Spirituall *Observations*, Generall and Particular by the *Authour*, of chiefe and fpeciall ufe (upon all occafions,) to all the *Englifh* Inhabiting thofe parts ; yet pleafant and profitable to the view of all men :

BY ROGER WILLIAMS
of *Providence* in *New-England.*

LONDON,
Printed by *Gregory Dexter,* 1643.

EDUCATION IN NEW ENGLAND

The New England settlers placed great value on education, which was the means of spreading Puritan beliefs and uniting the community. Religious and moral education was available to settlers through their schools and churches. Printing developed alongside education, because many of the colonists knew how to read. Printed material was another way of spreading Puritan teachings throughout the colony. The Puritan leaders were concerned that there would not be enough educated ministers for their churches. In 1636 they established a small college in the town of Cambridge, Massachusetts, which was named after John Harvard, its chief benefactor.

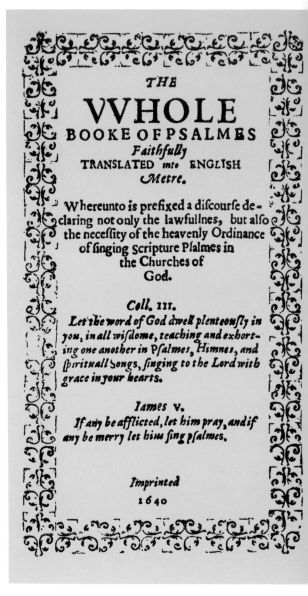

THE
VVHOLE
BOOKE OF PSALMES
Faithfully
TRANSLATED into ENGLISH
Metre.

Whereunto is prefixed a difcourse de-
claring not only the lawfulnes, but alfo
the neceffity of the heavenly Ordinance
of finging Scripture Pfalmes in
the Churches of
God.

Coll. III.
*Let the word of God dwell plenteoufly in
you, in all wifdome, teaching and exhort-
ing one another in Pfalmes, Himnes, and
fpirituall Songs, finging to the Lord with
grace in your hearts.*

Iames V.
*If any be afflicted, let him pray, and if
any be merry let him fing pfalmes.*

Imprinted
1640

The Whole Book of Psalmes *(above), also known as the "Bay Psalm Book," was the first book printed in America and was widely read by the New England settlers. Stephen Daye, a printer in Cambridge, brought it out in 1640.*

In the early days of Harvard College students often paid their tuition in livestock. The normal course of study lasted four years. Students who wished to become ministers would stay for three more years. This illustration (above) shows a view of the campus in the early 1700s.

John Cotton (1585-1652; right) was an important Puritan minister and teacher who came to Massachusetts in 1633. Almost at once he became pastor of the First Church of Boston, a post he held until his death. His sermons became famous for their powerful messages, and Cotton attracted a large following in the Boston community.

Part II: 1650-1754
Change and Conflict

George Whitefield (1714-70) was an evangelistic preacher from England and a leader of what would become the Calvinist Methodist Church. He first came to America in 1738, where he was an influential figure in the Great Awakening.

The period beginning in 1651 was a time of growth and expansion for the colonies. Through enormous land grants to its subjects, the English crown gained more and more territory in North America. The colonies stretched in an unbroken line along the Atlantic coast from New England to the Carolinas by the middle of the eighteenth century.

Colonial leaders gradually learned how to use the tools necessary for self-government. For the most part, colonial governments cooperated with England during this period and ruled their districts with little interference from their sovereigns. Even so, colonists began to protest trade restrictions imposed from England. These restrictions were designed to protect England's interests at its European rivals' expense.

Political and religious changes in Europe affected colonial communities during this period. In 1646, the English king, Charles I, was deposed. Three years later, he was beheaded by order of Parliament under the Puritan leadership of Oliver Cromwell. Cromwell then took over the rule of England as Protector. Puritans in New England welcomed the event, which seemed to support their mission to the rest of the world. Threatened by the arrival of other religious groups from all over Europe, Puritan leaders responded with persecution, sometimes even trying and punishing their own people.

These pressures and changes set the stage for the Great Awakening, a religious revival of the 1730s that seemed to meet a tremendous popular need. The colonists sought inspiration and a new sense of purpose. Religious leaders such as Jonathan Edwards and George Whitefield reached out to them with powerful and moving words.

A TIMELINE OF MAJOR EVENTS

PART II *1650-1754 Change and Conflict*

1650-1669

WORLD HISTORY

1651 Charles II, son of Charles I, is crowned king of Scotland; after unsuccessfully invading England, he flees to France.

1652 England declares war on Holland.

1654 The Treaty of Westminster ends the First Anglo-Dutch War.

1659 The Peace of the Pyrenees ends the war between France and Spain; Spanish power gradually declines while France becomes the dominant power in Europe.

1660 The monarchy is restored in England, with Charles II as king.

1661 Cardinal Mazarin, the prime minister of France, dies at Vincennes.

1664 The Second Anglo-Dutch War breaks out.

1666 London is almost destroyed by fire.

1667 France invades the Spanish Netherlands.

1668 England, Holland, and Sweden form the Triple Alliance to oppose France's seizure of the Spanish Netherlands.

The Great Fire of London

COLONIAL HISTORY **GOVERNMENT**

1650 England's first Navigation Act gives the nation's merchants a monopoly on trade with its colonies; the law also requires colonists to sell their products only to England and to ship them aboard English vessels.

1651 The colonies are caught up in the English Civil War; in Virginia, Governor William Berkeley is forced to surrender to a Parliamentary fleet.

1652 Massachusetts declares itself a self-governing commonwealth; New England, being mostly Puritan, supports the Parliamentary cause in England.

1653 Peter Stuyvesant allows some local government in New Amsterdam, but says his power to rule comes "from God and the company, not a few ignorant citizens."

1658 The first colonial police force is organized in New Amsterdam.

1660 Virginia passes the first of many laws defining the status of slavery and depriving slaves of legal rights; most other colonies adopt similar "slave codes." Dutch traders had brought the first slaves to Virginia in 1619.

1663 Another Navigation Act strengthens England's monopoly on colonial trade.

1664 Non-members of Puritan churches are permitted to vote in Massachusetts if they own property there.

1665 With New Amsterdam now in England's hands, representatives from Dutch and English settlements meet to draft a legal code for the colony.

COLONIAL HISTORY **RELIGION AND EDUCATION**

1650 Settlements in Connecticut set educational standards similar to those in Massachusetts.

1654 The first Jews arrive in the Dutch colony of New Amsterdam.
• The Toleration Act is repealed in Maryland during political turmoil, but is later reinstated.

1656 Quakers begin to appear in the colonies; they are persecuted for their beliefs both in New Netherland and New England, and four are hanged in Boston.

Quakers are persecuted

1663 Rhode Island's charter includes a law protecting religious freedom.
• John Eliot completes his translation of the Bible into the Algonquian Indian language; it is the first Bible published in North America in any language.

1665 Jesuit missionary Claude Allouez arrives in New France; for nearly a quarter of a century he oversees growing missionary efforts in the Great Lakes region and other parts of New France.

1667 A Virginia law states that a slave's baptism or conversion to Christianity "doth not alter the condition of the person as to his bondage or freedome."

A slave auction poster

1678 Rumors of a "Popish Plot" to restore Catholicism in England lead to anti-Catholic persecutions and laws.

1685 Louis XIV of France revokes the Edict of Nantes, renewing conflict between French Catholics and Protestants.

1686 Catholic European nations ally as the League of Augsburg to oppose France's plans for expansion.

King Louis XIV

1688 In the bloodless "Glorious Revolution," England's Catholic King James II is overthrown; he is replaced by his Protestant Dutch son-in-law William III, who rules jointly with Queen Mary.

1689 The English Parliament passes a Declaration of Rights, limiting royal power and prohibiting Catholics from ruling.
• Peter the Great becomes czar of Russia

and brings European ideas and technology to that nation.
• War of the Grand Alliance breaks out, pitting France against the coalition of states (including England and Spain) that make up the League of Augsburg.

1697 The Treaty of Ryswick ends the War of the Grand Alliance; there is no clear winner, but France gives up some territory.

1670 The great political philosopher John Locke writes the fundamental constitutions, setting up the legal framework

John Locke

for English settlements in the Carolinas.
• New Jersey colonists rebel against Governor Philip Carteret when he tries to collect rents on land for the colony's government.

1676 Bacon's Rebellion flares in Virginia; western planters march on Jamestown to protest what they feel is lack of protection from Indian attacks. Jamestown is burned, but the revolt collapses when leader

Nathaniel Bacon falls ill and dies.

1687 To assert royal authority, Royal Governor Sir Edmund Andros demands Connecticut's original charter; according to some accounts, colonists hide the charter in a hollow oak tree in Hartford to frustrate Andros.

1691 Maryland becomes a royal colony.

1696 Parliament passes another Navigation Act, setting up a board of trade to oversee commerce with the colonies.

1697 William Penn proposes a congress with representatives from all the colonies.

1699 Virginia's capital is moved from Jamestown to Williamsburg.

1671 Quaker leader George Fox begins a missionary journey through the colonies.

1674 There are fourteen villages of "Praying Indians"—Indians who had converted to Christianity—in New England; however, many are killed or driven out of the region during King Philip's War, 1675-76.

1682 Pennsylvania's "Frame of Government"

SOUTH WEST ELEVATION

Old Ship Meeting House 1681

guarantees religious freedom; as a result the colony becomes a haven for Quakers and members of other religious minorities.

1688 Quakers in Pennsylvania advocate the abolition of slavery in the colonies.

1690 The New England Primer, the best-known colonial schoolbook, is published in Boston.

1693 Witchcraft hysteria

in Salem, Massachusetts, results in the death of twenty suspected "witches"; many of the Puritan clergymen who presided over the trials and executions later express regret at the incident.

1695 The first synagogue in North America is founded in New York.

Change and Conflict **35**

A TIMELINE OF MAJOR EVENTS

PART II *1650-1754 Change and Conflict*

1 7 0 0 - 1 7 3 5

WORLD HISTORY

1701 The question of who will rule Spain and its empire leads to the War of the Spanish Succession; eventually, Spain and France are opposed by England, Holland, and several other states.
• Frederick, ruler of Brandenburg, becomes Frederick I, the first king of Prussia.

1704 Forces led by England's Duke of

The Duke of Marlborough

Marlborough win a major victory over France and Spain in the Battle of Blenheim.

1707 England and Scotland are united as Great Britain.

1713 The Treaty of Utrecht ends the War of the Spanish Succession.

1714 Queen Anne of England dies and is succeeded by the German George I, elector of Hanover and a great-grandson of James I.

1718 England declares war on Spain; France

Seal of the Mississippi Co.

follows a year later.

1720 France's treasury is bankrupted after the Mississippi Company is revealed to be a sham.

1727 Spain's seizure of Gibraltar sparks a new war between that nation

COLONIAL HISTORY GOVERNMENT

1702 Delaware sets up a government separate from Pennsylvania.

1702 Queen Anne's War (in Europe called the New War of Spanish Succession) brings fighting in Canada between French and English colonists.

1704 The New York Assembly seizes power from the royal governor.

1712 North Carolina separates from South Carolina and gets its own governor.

1718 The French under Governor Sieur de

A French colonial cottage

Bienville found New Orleans on the Gulf of Mexico at the termination of the great Mississippi River. French settlements in Louisiana flourish until 1729 when wars with several Indian tribes erupt.

1733 The first settlers arrive in Georgia; James Oglethorpe, their leader, hopes the colony will provide a place "for the industrious yet unfortunate poor."

1734 John Peter Zenger, publisher of the *New York Weekly Journal*, is arrested for printing articles criticizing New York's governor, William Cosby.

1735 After a landmark trial, John Peter Zenger is released from prison; the case is an important step in assuring freedom of the press in America.

COLONIAL HISTORY RELIGION AND EDUCATION

1700 The College of William and Mary in Virginia begins granting degrees.

1701 The Vestry Act makes the Church of England the established (official) church in North Carolina; the Church of England, also known as the Anglican and later the Episcopal Church, is established in most other southern colonies.

1706 The increase in Scottish and Scots-Irish immigration to the English colonies leads to the founding of the Presbyterian Church in Philadelphia.
• Mennonites, members of a religious sect from Germany, begin settling in Pennsylvania.

1707 Five Pennsylvania churches join to form the first Baptist association in the colonies.

1717 John Wise's *A Vindication of the Government of the New England Churches* defends the "congregational" organization or New England Puritanism.
• Puritan minister Cotton Mather opens a night school for blacks and Indians.

1730 The first Masonic Lodge in the colonies is founded in Philadelphia.

1731 Benjamin Franklin

starts a circulating library in Philadelphia; it is a forerunner of today's public libraries.

1734 The Great Awakening—a religious revival that eventually sweeps the colonies— begins in New England.
• The Salzburgers, Lutheran refugees from Salzburg in Austria, arrive in Georgia.

and Britain.

1739 Frederick II, "the Great," becomes king of Prussia.

1740 The War of the

Frederick II of Prussia

Austrian Succession begins in Europe.

Maria Theresa of Austria

Charles Edward Stuart, grandson of James II, lands in Scotland in a bid to restore Britain to Stuart rule.

1746 Stuart supporters, called Jacobites, are defeated in the Battle of Culloden.

1748 The War of the Austrian Succession ends with the Treaty of Aix-la-Chapelle.

The Battle of Culloden

1737 Jews are denied the right to vote in New York.

1740 Parliament passes laws for the naturalization of immigrants to the colonies; they can become British subjects after seven years' residence.

1740 During the War of Jenkins Ear between Spain and England, Ogelthorpe invades Florida. Spain, in turn invades Georgia.

1744 King George's War breaks out in North America between English colonists and French colonists and their Indian allies. New Englanders succeed in capturing Fort Louisburg on Cape Breton Island (1747) but fail to take Montreal and Quebec (1747). The war ends in 1748 with Fort Louisburg being returned to the French.

1747 The New York Bar Association, the first

legal society in the colonies, is founded.

1753 The Liberty Bell is first rung to call a meeting of the Pennsylvania Assembly; the bell (which cracked during testing) bears a verse from the Bible: "Proclaim Liberty throughout all the land unto all the inhabitants thereof."

1754 In Albany, New York, Benjamin Franklin proposes that

the colonies—along with the Iroquois Confederacy—unite for defense against the French and their Indian allies.

A cartoon urging unity

1737 Jonathan Edwards, one of the major figures in the Great Awakening, publishes his *Narrative of the Surprising Works of God*. John Wesley (later, with his brother Charles, the founder of Methodism) arrives in Georgia to serve as the colony's chaplain.

1739 Moravians, members of a German religious sect, begin arriving in Georgia; most later move to

Pennsylvania.
• George Whitefield, one of the major figures of the Great Awakening, preaches to huge crowds throughout the colonies.

1742 Henry Melchior Muhlenberg arrives in Pennsylvania; he becomes the major leader of the colony's Lutherans.

1746 Presbyterians found the College of New Jersey (later

Princeton) to train ministers.

King's College

1749 Moravians found two schools for girls, at Lititz and Bethlehem, Pennsylvania. (Formal education in the colonies was mostly limited to boys.)

1754 King's College (later Columbia University) is founded in New York City.
•Jonathan Edwards publishes *Inquiry into the Freedom of the Will*, one of the most influential works of theology by an American.

Jonathan Edwards

RELIGION IN EUROPE: THE STRUGGLE FOR FREEDOM

Many groups came to the New World to escape religious persecution in Europe. These people interpreted and practiced Christianity in ways that angered and threatened both the traditional Roman Catholic and Protestant churches. One such group was the Moravians, a religious movement that began in the fifteenth century in Eastern Europe. Constant attacks drove them westward, and the religious wars of the seventeenth century almost wiped them out. In 1722, the Moravians arrived in the German province of Saxony, where a wealthy landowner gave them refuge and allowed them to build a town. Moravians began coming to America in 1735. They ultimately settled in Pennsylvania, where they founded the town of Bethlehem.

The Religious Society of Friends, also known as the Quakers, was another group that thrived after emigrating to the colonies. The Quaker movement began in England in the mid-1600s and caused much controversy by stating that individual worshipers could contact God directly, without either rituals or ministers. The Quakers, too, suffered mistreatment because of their beliefs. The violence against them drove them to America, where they first arrived in Massachusetts in 1656. They settled in Pennsylvania, the colony founded by William Penn, himself a Quaker.

In this nineteenth-century engraving (above), sixteenth-century Moravian farmers face an attack by Catholics. Constant cruel attacks such as this almost wiped out the Moravians until they found a protector in the Saxon Count Zinzendorf. Ultimately, they prospered in the New World.

The Quakers usually worshiped in silence, but those who wished to speak aloud, if "moved by the spirit," could do so at any time. This illustration (above) shows a Quaker meeting in France in the mid-1700s.

WILLIAM PENN AND THE FOUNDING OF PENNSYLVANIA

William Penn joined the Society of Friends (Quakers) while managing his family's estates in Ireland in the late 1660s. In 1690, he inherited most of his father's money and began working as a missionary in Europe. His converts began emigrating to America to escape persecution, and Penn used his wealth and influence to assist them. In 1681, Penn was granted a large tract of land on the Delaware River from King Charles II, as payment for a debt the Crown owed Penn's father, an admiral. The following year, Penn brought a group of colonists to his land, which he named Pennsylvania after his father. He wrote a constitution for the new "commonwealth" that set up a democratic form of government and included a bill of rights guaranteeing religious freedom. Penn himself laid out the plans for the city of Philadelphia and negotiated a series of treaties that established friendly relations between the Quakers and the Delaware Indians for years to come. Before long, Pennsylvania became famous as a haven for religious groups that were not welcome in other communities. The Quakers established schools and hospitals in their new community and continued to speak out strongly against slavery and warfare.

William Penn (1644-1718; above) helped found three colonies in the New World— Pennsylvania, New Jersey, and Delaware. A devout Quaker and an influential leader, Penn spent time in prison for his beliefs while he lived in England. His strong support for religious freedom set an important standard for the colonies.

William Penn's pamphlet, Some Account of the Province of Pennsilvania *(right), offered a description of the countryside along with advice and information for anyone wishing to emigrate there. Excerpts from the colony's Royal Charter were also printed in the pamphlet.*

In 1684, Penn returned to England, where he became entangled in political disputes. He did not return to Philadelphia until 1699, when he moved into the slate-roofed house pictured below.

SOME
ACCOUNT
OF THE
PROVINCE
OF
PENNSILVANIA
IN
AMERICA;
Lately Granted under the Great Seal
OF
ENGLAND
TO
William Penn, &c.

Together with Priviledges and Powers necessary to the well-governing thereof.

Made publick for the Information of such as are or may be disposed to Transport themselves or Servants into those Parts.

LONDON: Printed, and Sold by *Benjamin Clark* Bookseller in *George-Yard Lombard-street,* 1681.

TYRANNY AND REBELLION

In contrast to William Penn's liberal ideals, there were some colonial administrators who believed in harsh and autocratic methods of governing. After enemies of the Massachusetts Bay Colony had persuaded the king to cancel its charter, Sir Edmund Andros was appointed royal English governor of New England in 1686. Andros then incorporated Massachusetts into a Dominion of New England. He made a number of unpopular changes, including limiting the power of local governments, imposing new taxes, and challenging land claims. These changes presented a major threat to the authority the Puritans had established. Before long, complaints against Andros reached the English Parliament. Encouraged by sympathy from England, the people of Massachusetts rebelled against Andros's rule. On April 18, 1689, he was overthrown and imprisoned.

Another unpopular colonial leader was Peter Stuyvesant, who governed the Dutch colony of New Amsterdam from 1647 to 1664. He established a council of nine advisers, but he almost immediately dissolved it when the advisers approached the Dutch government with their grievances. Stuyvesant was an enemy of the Quakers and other religious minorities and encouraged cruel treatment of them.

Sir Edmund Andros (1637-1714; above) brought about his own downfall by trying to limit the power of colonial governments that had been protected in previous charters granted by the English crown. After he was overthrown in 1689, Andros was sent back to England, but no charges were ever brought against him.

Peter Stuyvesant (c. 1610-72) lost his authority over New Amsterdam in 1664, when an English naval fleet arrived and demanded the colony's surrender. At first, the governor refused, as shown in this nineteenth-century illustration (right). But after realizing that his defenses were too weak to drive off the English warships, Stuyvesant turned the Dutch settlement over to England.

THE INDIANS AND CHRISTIANITY

The Europeans who came to the New World were often frightened and alarmed by the religions and customs of the Native Americans they encountered. Converting the Indians to Christianity was an important goal for colonial governments. The Puritans would convert those Indians who were willing, in the belief that they were bringing God's word to the wilderness. Some colonial leaders only wanted influence over the Indians in order to gain control of their land, but others wished to convert the Indians to Christianity. One such leader was John Eliot, a pastor who came to Roxbury, Massachusetts in 1631. Eliot studied the Algonquian language in order to preach to the Algonquin-speaking tribes, and in the course of his career he established six churches and a ministry that included Indians.

Another Christian group that was active in efforts to convert the Indians of North America was the Jesuits, a Roman Catholic order whose first missionaries came to the New World with the Spanish explorations in the sixteenth century. Determined to convert the Indians to Roman Catholicism, Jesuit missionaries learned to speak several Indian languages and traveled into the wilderness beyond the French settlements in Canada and the Great Lakes region.

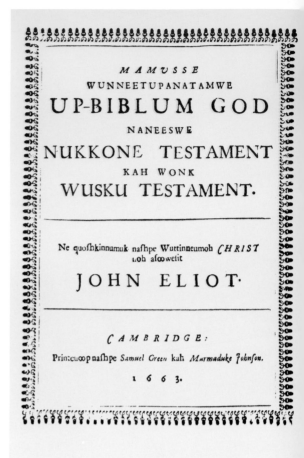

Known as "the Apostle to the Indians," John Eliot (1604-90) spent most of his life trying to convert the Indians of New England to Christianity. In order to make the Holy Scripture available to them, Eliot translated the entire English Bible into the Algonquian language. The Algonquian title page is shown here (above). In 1663, the Cambridge Press printed 1,500 copies of the book, the first Indian Bible ever published in North America.

Eliot wanted to convert the Indians to Christianity so that "they may be the Lord's people ruled by Him alone in all things." He is pictured in this illustration (above) from a nineteenth-century history book delivering a sermon to a gathering of Algonquian-speaking Indians. In 1660, Eliot established the first church for Indians in Massachusetts.

In this nineteenth-century engraving (left), a Jesuit missionary addresses a gathering of Indians in the territory of New France. Many Indians were willing to integrate elements of Christianity into their own religions, but some groups found it hard to accept the idea of there being only one supreme God.

THE SALEM WITCHCRAFT TRIALS

Puritans, like most people at the time, believed in the existence of witches. Because witches were thought to possess destructive, magical powers, they were greatly feared in New England, but the witch hysteria did not take hold until 1692. In that year, in the town of Salem, Massachusetts, a teenage girl went into convulsions after an argument with a servant. When the girl's brother and sister also complained of aches and pains, the townspeople were convinced that the servant, an elderly woman, was a witch. Although she claimed innocence, the woman was imprisoned and hanged.

Many similar incidents followed. In most cases, the accusers were teenagers or children who could have been ill, leading the town to believe they were bewitched. The governor of Massachusetts, Sir William Phips, set up a special court to investigate the matter. The judges, under pressure from the community to deliver harsh punishments, often convicted the accused on no evidence other than the testimony of the witnesses. Fourteen women and six men were executed. But when prominent citizens, among them Phips's wife and some of Mather's relatives, were accused, officials began to question the court's procedures. The special court was dissolved in September 1692, and the 150 prisoners awaiting trial were released.

This Puritan meeting house (above), one of the oldest still standing in New England, was built in Hingham, Massachusetts, in 1681. An important part of any Puritan settlement, the meeting house was the only place where all the townspeople gathered every day. Puritan churches were always simple in design, unlike the elaborately decorated cathedrals and churches of the Church of England, which Puritans considered too similar to those of the Roman Catholic Church. The Puritans believed that beauty and riches could tempt men and women to sin, and so they stressed simplicity in their dress and architecture.

This highly imaginative version of a witch trial (right) was drawn in 1892, 200 years after the events at Salem. The young woman appeals to Satan to save her, and with a bolt of lightning her chains are broken, while one of the judges collapses in a faint before the stand. No such incident ever took place during the actual trials.

Change and Conflict **47**

ADVANCES AND CHANGES IN EDUCATION

Education for children was highly valued in New England. In 1657, the Massachusetts Bay Colony passed a law requiring towns of fifty or more families to hire a schoolmaster. The schoolroom was an important place for children to learn proper behavior, and schoolbooks were written to teach young readers to fear and respect God.

Toward the end of the 1600s and into the 1700s, prosperous citizens turned to education as a means both to learn the customs and ways of gentlemen and to gain skills in business. Benjamin Franklin (1706-90), a statesman and writer who lived in Philadelphia, was especially concerned with education, arguing that only with sound, proper schooling could young men become useful members of a prosperous and free society. Although the literacy rate for women was relatively high in New England, most formal education was intended only for men.

The church remained an important force in founding schools and colleges. Harvard College was founded by Puritans in 1636, and in 1701 the Congregational Church granted a charter to establish a college in Connecticut, which was later named after Elihu Yale, its chief benefactor. Yale College was originally a school for clergymen, but in the course of the eighteenth century, other courses of study were added to the program.

Yale College, shown in this view from the early nineteenth century (below), was originally established in the town of Killingworth, Connecticut. In 1716 it was moved to its present-day location, in the city of New Haven.

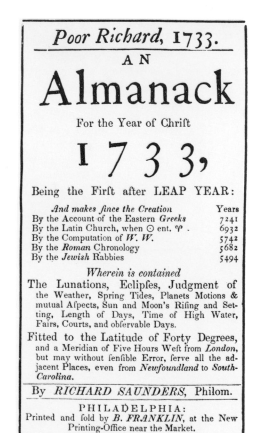

Poor Richard, 1733.

AN

Almanack

For the Year of Chrift

1733,

Being the Firft after LEAP YEAR:

And makes fince the Creation   Years
By the Account of the Eastern *Greeks*   7241
By the Latin Church, when ☉ ent. ♈ .   6932
By the Computation of *W. W.*   5742
By the *Roman* Chronology   5682
By the *Jewish* Rabbies   5494

Wherein is contained

The Lunations, Eclipfes, Judgment of the Weather, Spring Tides, Planets Motions & mutual Afpects, Sun and Moon's Rifing and Setting, Length of Days, Time of High Water, Fairs, Courts, and obfervable Days.

Fitted to the Latitude of Forty Degrees, and a Meridian of Five Hours Weft from *London*, but may without fenfible Error, ferve all the adjacent Places, even from *Newfoundland* to *South-Carolina*.

By *RICHARD SAUNDERS*, Philom.

PHILADELPHIA:

Printed and fold by *B. FRANKLIN*, at the New Printing-Office near the Market.

Poor Richard's Almanack *(left) was first published in 1732 by Benjamin Franklin, and was one of many contributions Franklin made to colonial education. Almanacs were books that contained practical information about weather, farming, and medicine. Franklin's annually published almanac was especially popular for both its humor and wisdom.*

GEOGRAPHY

EPITOMIZED;

J. Bloomfield

OR, A

Tour round the World.

BEING

A SHORT BUT COMPREHENSIVE

DESCRIPTION

Q129
D25
OF THE

TERRAQUEOUS GLOBE,

ATTEMPTED IN VERSE,

FOR THE SAKE OF THE MEMORY.

And principally defigned for the Ufe of

SCHOOLS.

By ROBERT DAVIDSON.

===

BURLINGTON:
PRINTED BY NEALE & LAWRENCE.
M.DCC.XCI.

Books for children in the colonial period were often meant to instruct, not entertain, the reader. Stories for children usually delivered a moral message: good acts were rewarded, while acts of mischief were punished, often by the hand of God. The History of Little Goody Twoshoes (opposite page, right) tells the story of a pious, hardworking woman who is properly rewarded for her virtues.

This textbook (above), published in Philadelphia in 1784, provided schoolchildren with descriptions of the countries and continents around the world. The author, Robert Davidson, composed the text entirely in verse so that students could memorize the information more easily. An excerpt reads:

A-going a-going, we'll set off in style
The wonders of Asia to see;
We'll take our farewell of Old England awhile,
And give a good jump o'er the sea.

As colonial towns grew and thrived in the 1700s, citizens became more interested in acquiring knowledge and making books available to the public. The Redwood Library (opposite page, right) was built in Newport, Rhode Island, in 1748. The library was a reflection of the success Newport's citizens were enjoying in the shipbuilding and slave trades.

Goody Twoshoes.

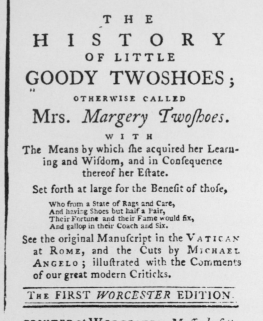

THE
HISTORY
OF LITTLE
GOODY TWOSHOES;
OTHERWISE CALLED
Mrs. *Margery Twoshoes.*
WITH
The Means by which she acquired her Learn-
ing and Wisdom, and in Consequence
thereof her Estate.

Set forth at large for the Benefit of those,

Who from a State of Rags and Care,
And having Shoes but half a Pair,
Their Fortune and their Fame would fix,
And gallop in their Coach and Six.

See the original Manuscript in the VATICAN
at ROME, and the Cuts by MICHAEL
ANGELO; illustrated with the Comments
of our great modern Criticks.

THE FIRST *WORCESTER* EDITION.

PRINTED at WORCESTER, *Massachusetts.*
By ISAIAH THOMAS,
And SOLD, Wholesale and Retail, at his Book
Store. MDCCXXXVII.

THE GREAT AWAKENING

As the colonies grew in the 1700s, many people began straying away from the church, distracted by the promise of wealth and property. Others felt a great need for a revival of religious feeling, and they flocked to inspirational meetings and sermons by such ministers as Jonathan Edwards and John Wesley. The ministers warned their congregations to either repent their sins and lead pious lives or face God's wrath. The preachers' vivid descriptions of hell caused great excitement and fear among the people, leading more and more settlers to attend meetings and return to church. This period, known as the Great Awakening, reached its peak in 1739 when George Whitefield, a founder of the Methodist church, set out on a two-year tour of the colonies, during which he preached to thousands of people. Many new colleges were founded as a result of the Great Awakening, including Princeton in 1746, King's College (later Columbia) in 1754, and Dartmouth College in 1769.

When George Whitefield first came to America from England in 1738, he became involved in raising money for this orphanage (below) in Bethesda, Georgia. He toured the colonies the next year, going north along the Atlantic coast from Georgia to New England. His deeply inspiring sermons brought in not only contributions but a large following of believers as well.

Jonathan Edwards (1703-1758; right) was a minister of the Congregational Church who led the Great Awakening in Massachusetts. He graduated from Yale at the age of 17 in 1720. Although he had strong interests in science, literature, and philosophy, Edwards considered the study of God's word the most important branch of learning. In 1729, Edwards took charge of the congregation of Northampton, Massachusetts, where his grandfather had been a minister. His brilliant sermons soon attracted a large following in New England, and by 1735 he was admitting thirty converts a week into his church.

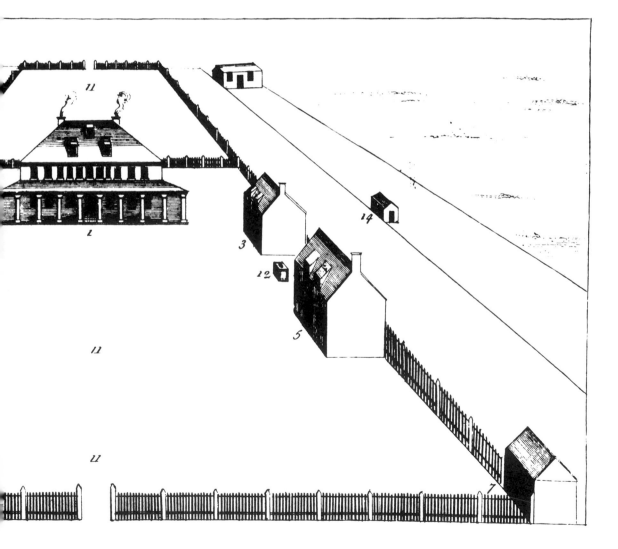

RELIGIOUS FREEDOM AND DIVERSITY

The settlements that welcomed different religious groups were often those that had themselves been founded in the name of religious freedom. Roger Williams founded Rhode Island when the Puritan leaders forced him to leave Massachusetts Bay in 1636. Twenty–two years later, in 1658, the first Jewish families came there seeking religious freedom and settled in the town of Newport. Although they were allowed to take part in Newport's thriving economy, the Jews had no vote in the town's affairs. They met in private homes until 1758, when they chose a permanent rabbi, Isaac Touro, and built a synagogue.

The Anglican Church, also known as the Church of England, had been established in the southern colonies by the mid-1700s. The Puritans of New England did not welcome Anglican settlers, having long since broken with the Church of England. The Anglicans were able to come to Philadelphia, however, which prided itself on guaranteeing personal and religious freedom.

Named after the first permanent rabbi in Newport, the Touro Synagogue was consecrated in 1763. It is the oldest synagogue in America. This view (right) shows the interior, designed with the Holy Ark facing east toward Jerusalem. The chandelier is more than 450 years old.

Christ's Church (below) was founded by Anglicans in Philadelphia in 1723. The building's ornate classical style, derived from churches in England, differs greatly from the simple meeting houses of the Puritans.

COLONIAL TREATIES WITH THE INDIANS

An important task of colonial governments was to negotiate treaties with the Native Americans, usually for the purpose of gaining Indian land for growing settlements. Sometimes colonial leaders conducted these discussions fairly. In other cases they took advantage of their Indian counterparts. Misunderstandings and poor communication due to language differences often caused hostility and bitterness between the two groups, as in the case of the Walking Purchase. This agreement was signed in Pennsylvania in August 1737 by the Delaware Indians and Thomas Penn, son of William Penn. The treaty gave to the Pennsylvania colonists all the land that could be covered on foot in one day and a half. The colonists supposedly walked as fast as they could, covering thirty miles in the first six hours of the journey. The Delawares, led by Chief Lappawinsoe, were shocked by this behavior. They had expected the white men to pace out the land with "deliberation, and to rest and smoke by the way."

Lappawinsoe was chief of the Delaware Indians at the time of the Walking Purchase. After the agreement was signed, he was reported to have said that "They [the colonists] had got all the best of the land, and they might go to the Devil for the bad, and that he would send no Indians with them." This illustration (above) is based on a portrait that was painted by Gustavus Hesselius in about 1735.

The calumet, or peace pipe, had a long, feathered stem and did not always include a pipe bowl. Such pipes were considered sacred and were usually smoked to seal treaties or agreements. In this drawing (right) of a calumet ceremony from a seventeenth-century book, the Indians are waiting in a circle for the arrival of the chief who is carrying the pipe. Following him are Indians from neighboring villages, who are participating in the ceremony as a gesture of friendship.

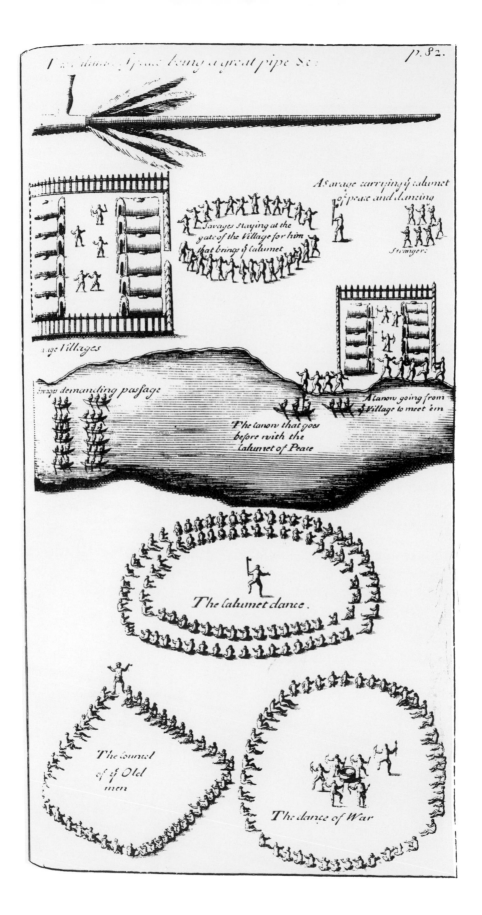

The Calumet of Peace being a great pipe &c.

p. 82.

A savage carrying ye calumet of peace and dancing

Savages staying at the gate of the village for him that brings ye calumet

Strangers

Savage Villages

Savages demanding passage

A canow going from ye Village to meet 'em

The canow that goes before with the calumet of Peace

The calumet dance.

The Counsel of ye Old men

The dance of War

THE ALBANY PLAN

The Albany Plan, drafted in 1754, sought to unify English colonies in America under a central government. It was drafted in 1754, in response to fears that without this central authority, the English colonies would not be able to defend themselves against French or Indian attacks. Each colony would retain its separate authority, but the new government would have broad powers over taxation, Indian affairs, and military matters. The new administration would be overseen by a president-general—to be appointed by the king—and a council of delegates from the colonies. The Albany Plan was approved by the colonial delegates, among them Benjamin Franklin. But it was rejected by King George II, who feared that the union would undermine English authority in America. The plan was also turned down by the colonial legislatures, which believed it would threaten the power of each individual colony. Although it never became a reality, the Albany Plan was an important step toward colonial unity.

The Iroquois Confederacy, founded in the sixteenth century, was the most powerful Indian alliance in the colonies. This map (below) shows the territories of the five original tribes of the Confederacy: Mohawk, Seneca, Cayuga, Onondaga, and Oneida. Although this example of Indian unity and strength was threatening to some of the delegates who drew up the Albany Plan, others suggested inviting the Iroquois to join the proposed coalition.

JOIN, or DIE.

This cartoon (left), one of the first in the history of American journalism, appeared in the Pennsylvania Gazette *with an article by Benjamin Franklin promoting the Albany Plan. The woodcut shows a snake cut into parts, representing the different colonies. Franklin argued that, like a living creature, the colonies would not survive unless they were joined together.*

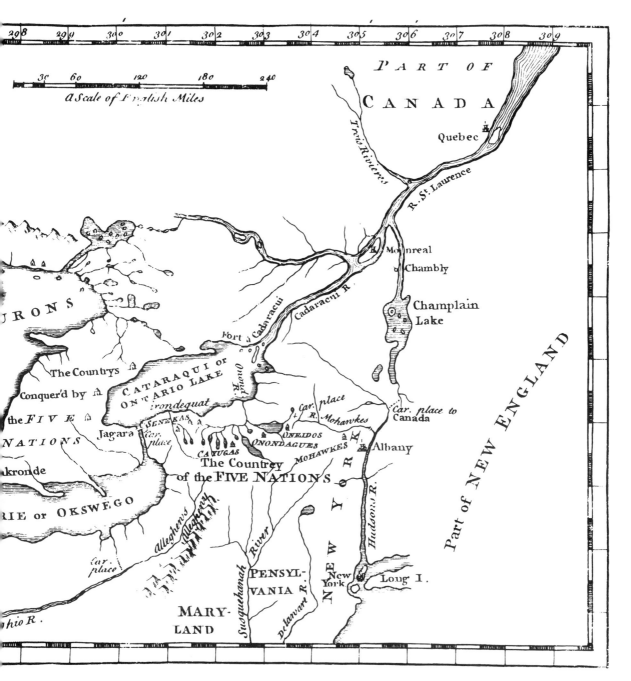

The BLOODY MASSACRE perpetrated in King-Street Boston on March 5th 1770 by a party of the 29th REG.

Engrav'd Printed & Sold by PAUL REVERE BOSTON

Unhappy Boston! see thy Sons deplore,
Thy hallow'd Walks besmear'd with guiltless Gore
While faithless P—n and his savage Bands,
With murd'rous Rancour stretch their bloody Hands,
Like fierce Barbarians grinning o'er their Prey,
Approve the Carnage, and enjoy the Day.

If scalding drops from Rage from Anguish Wrung
If speechless Sorrows lab'ring for a Tongue
Or if a weeping World can ought appease
The plaintive Ghosts of Victims such as these:
The Patriot's copious Tears for each are shed,
A glorious Tribute which embalms the Dead.

But know Fate summons to that awful Goal
Where Justice strips the Murd'rer of his Soul
Should venal C—ts the scandal of the Land,
Snatch the relentless Villain from her Hand,
Keen Execrations on this Plate inscrib'd
Shall reach a Judge who never can be brib'd.

The unhappy Sufferers were Mess[rs] Sam[l] Gray Sam[l] Maverick, Jam[s] Caldwell, Crispus Attucks & Pat[k] Carr
Killed. Six wounded; two of them (Christ[r] Monk & John Clark) Mortally

Published in 1770 by Paul Revere Boston

This period of colonial history begins immediately after the start of the French and Indian War, the seven-year struggle between Britain and France over their territories in North America. American colonial soldiers fought alongside British troops against the French and their Indian allies. Peace was restored by the Treaty of Paris in 1763, which ceded almost all of France's territories in North America to Britain. The colonies were now firmly under British control.

Left with more territory to govern, along with a massive war debt, Parliament began considering ways to raise money. The most obvious method was to impose taxes on the colonies, which were allowed to trade only with Britain. These taxes would allow Britain to reap the benefits of its expanded holdings in the New World.

At first, the American colonists had no wish for complete independence from Britain. However, they had grown used to the benefits of self-government and prosperity, and they soon became resentful of Parliament's attempts to curb these freedoms. The new taxes raised a question that became one of the most important issues of the revolutionary period: Could Parliament be allowed to tax the colonists without giving them a voice in the British government?

The colonists who led protests against Britain were shrewd promoters of their cause. Through speeches, cartoons, broadsides (one-page announcements popular in the colonial period), and advertisements, they convinced much of the American public that Britain was determined to suppress the colonies. Many people realized that the only way to protect their rights and freedoms was to win complete independence from their British rulers.

The Boston Massacre resulted from tensions between British soldiers and the citizens of Boston. The townspeople resented the presence of the Redcoats, who were there to keep the peace amid an increasingly unruly public. On March 5, 1770, several incidents of fighting and harassment led the soldiers to fire on a crowd of citizens. The tragedy, which left five Bostonians dead, was exploited by revolutionary leaders to stir up anti-British sentiment. This illustration was engraved and published by Paul Revere shortly after the event.

A TIMELINE OF MAJOR EVENTS

PART III *1755-1775 The Struggle for Independence*

1755 · 1762

WORLD HISTORY

1756 Frederick the Great learns of a secret agreement between six European states (including France and Russia) to divide up Prussia between them; the Seven Years War begins with a Prussian attack on Austria; Britain allies itself with Prussia and declares war on France.
• William Pitt the Elder becomes Britain's Secretary of State; his vigorous leadership plays a major role in Britain's rise as a world power.

1757 Robert Clive establishes the rule of the British East India Company over most of India.

1759 The Royal Navy wins a string of worldwide sea battles; Britons call 1759 "The Glorious Year."

1760 George III becomes king of Great Britain following the death of his grandfather, George II.
• After years of back-and-forth fighting in Europe, Prussia suffers a series of battlefield defeats.
• French forces in India are defeated by the British, ending France's hope for a colonial empire in that region.

1761 Catherine II, "the Great," becomes Czarina of Russia.

Catherine II

1762 Britain captures many of Spain's Caribbean colonies, as well as the Philippines in the Pacific.

COLONIAL HISTORY GOVERNMENT

1755 The first major battle in the French and Indian War against the British colonies takes place in the Pennsylvania wilderness when a force led by British Major General Edward Braddock is ambushed and severely mauled. George Washington, an officer in the Virginia militia, is one of the survivors. The war lasts until the Treaty of Paris, in 1763.

Braddock's Retreat

1761 Britain passes a law requiring royal approval for all transfers of land between colonists and Indians. Another 1761 law allows the British government to reject nominees for colonial judgeships.
• Boston lawyer James Otis opposes the British practice of searching colonists' property (usually to look for smuggled goods) without search warrants.

COLONIAL HISTORY RELIGION AND EDUCATION

Presbyterian Theological Seminary, later Princeton University

1756 Jonathan Edwards is appointed president of the College of New Jersey, but dies shortly before taking office.

1758 Anglican missionaries in Philadelphia establish a school for African-American children.

1758 Touro Synagogue, serving a Jewish congregation in Newport, Rhode Island, is designed and built.

Touro Synagogue

1760 Students at the College of William and Mary protest the poor quality of the college's food in an early case of campus unrest.

1762 A collection of hymns is translated into the Delaware Indian language.
• The Moravian community at Bethlehem, Pennsylvania, ends a twenty-one-year experiment in communal living.

- Prussia, no longer an ally of Britain, makes peace with Austria.
- Jean-Jacques Rousseau publishes *The Social Contract*, a major work in the philosophical movement known as the Enlightenment.

1763 The Treaty of Paris ends the Seven Years' War, with Britain the clear winner.
- The British Parliament passes the Sugar Act, seeking to raise money to pay off war debts by taxing Britain's American colonies.

1764 The Currency Act forbids British colonies from printing their own paper money.

1765 Parliament passes the Stamp and Quartering acts; both are intended to pay for British troops stationed in North America.
- The British East India Company assumes control of the territory ruled by the emperors in India.
- Catherine the Great calls for modernization in Russia.

1767 Britain's Townshend Acts impose more taxes on the colonies.

1768 In one of a series of important voyages, British Captain James Cook explores and charts the coasts of Australia and New Zealand.

Captain James Cook

1763 The "Paxton Boys" riot takes place in Pennsylvania: Frontier settlers claim that the colony's government (which is dominated by pacifist Quakers) is not protecting them from Indian attack, and march on Philadelphia.

1764 James Otis writes *The Rights of the British Colonies Asserted and Proved* to protest the Sugar Act; many colonists also boycott British goods in protest.

- The "Regulator War" breaks out in the Carolinas; like other conflicts, it pits frontier settlers against officials in the eastern shore.

1765 The Stamp Act sparks the strongest colonial protest to date. A member of Parliament tells King George III the act "has made the blood of these sons of liberty boil within them." Representatives from most of the colonies meet in New York City to form a Stamp Act Congress; the congress formally protests the act to the king.
- The Quartering Act takes effect; British troops can now be lodged in private homes in the colonies, even against the owners' wishes.

1766 The Stamp Act is repealed, but the Declaratory Act—which asserts Britain's "sovereignty" in the colonies—is a new target of colonial protest.
- General Thomas Gage dissolves the New York Assembly after it refuses to obey the Quartering Act.

1768 James Otis and another prominent Massachusetts Patriot, Samuel Adams, circulate a letter throughout the colonies proposing united action against Britain.
- British troops and warships arrive in Boston.

1763 Spain expels Jesuit missionaries from Louisiana, which it gained in the French and Indian War.

1764 A fire at Harvard destroys much of the college's valuable laboratory equipment.
- The first Baptist college is founded at Warren, Rhode Island.

1765 The first medical school in North America is established as part of the College of Philadelphia.
- At least forty Latin schools (the colonial equivalent of modern high schools) are operating in Massachusetts.
- Boston clergyman Jonathan Mayhew's anti-British sermon, "Ye Have Been Called Unto Liberty," inspires a Patriot mob to burn a British official's house.

1767 Following disputes over the political power and wealth of the Jesuit order, Spain expels Jesuit missionaries from the southwest; they are replaced by friars of the Franciscan order.
- Sixty colonial Quaker leaders meet in Burlington, New Jersey; twenty-five of them are women.

1769 Junipero Serra, a Spanish Franciscan friar, founds the mission of San Diego de Alcala, the first mission in what will become California.
- Dartmouth College is founded in New Hampshire to train ministers for the Congregational Church.

Father Juniper Serra

1770 - 1773

WORLD HISTORY

Lord North

1770 Lord North becomes prime minister of Britain; he is determined to assert British control over the colonies.

The British Parliament

1772 Poland, formerly an independent nation, is divided between Russia, Austria, and Prussia.

1773 Parliament passes the Regulating Act, placing many functions of the British East India Company under control of the British government.

1773 Pope Clement XIV dissolves the Jesuit Order.

King George III

COLONIAL HISTORY **GOVERNMENT**

1770 British soldiers kill five members of a Boston mob in the "Boston Massacre"; in the resulting trial, the soldiers (who are represented by local lawyers, including John Adams) are cleared of murder charges.
• Parliament ends all the Townshend Act restrictions, except for a tax on tea.

1772 The royal governor

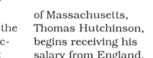

From a broadside published by Paul Revere

of Massachusetts, Thomas Hutchinson, begins receiving his salary from England, not from the colonists he governs; the colony's judges are soon placed

under the same policy.

1773 Parliament passes the Tea Act, giving British merchants a monopoly on the sale of tea to the colonies. In the best-known protest against the Tea Act, Boston Patriots dump tons of tea into the city harbor; similar actions and protests take place across the colonies. The Massachusetts Assembly asks Parliament to remove Royal Governor Thomas

Hutchinson from office.

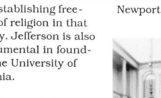

Patriots dump crates of tea into the Boston Harbor

COLONIAL HISTORY **RELIGION AND EDUCATION**

Thomas Jefferson

1770 Christoph Dock publishes the *Schul-Ordnung* to promote

public education among German immigrants in Pennsylvania.
• The College of Charleston is founded in South Carolina. Unlike most colonial colleges, it is sponsored by the community rather than a church, making it the forerunner of modern community colleges.
• Thomas Jefferson urges the Virginia Legislature to pass a

law establishing freedom of religion in that colony. Jefferson is also instrumental in founding the University of Virginia.

1771 Francis Asbury arrives in the colonies; he becomes the principal leader of American Methodists.

1773 The first Jewish sermon published in America (by Rabbi Haym Carregal of Touro Synagogue) is printed in

Newport, Rhode Island.

Interior of Touro Synoagogue

1774 Louis XVI becomes king of France.
• Parliament passes the Coercive Acts in an attempt to crush growing colonial resistance to British rule. Among their features, the Acts close the port of Boston and reduce the power of the Massachusetts legislature.

1775 Lord North extends the New England Restraining Act to South Carolina, Virginia, Pennsylvania, Maryland and New Jersey. The act forbids trade with any country other than Britain and Ireland, and will be bitterly resented.

Watt's steam engine

1775 Scottish inventor Isaac Watt develops an improved steam engine, Watt's invention encourages the growing Industrial Revolution in England. Watt sells his first steam engine to the industrialist John Wilkinson.

Edmund Burke

1775 British statesman Edmund Burke urges Parliament to compromise with the colonies, to no avail.

1774 In punishment for the Boston Tea Party, Parliament passes the Coercive Acts; the laws close the port of Boston and make the Massachusetts Assembly practically powerless.
• In May, Patriots in Rhode Island and Virginia call for a congress of representatives from all colonies.
• In June, Massachusetts calls for an intercolonial congress to meet in Philadelphia.

1774 In October, fifty-six delegates from twelve colonies form the First Continental Congress which meets in Philadelphia. The Congress drafts a list of complaints for King George III, formally organizes a boycott of commerce with Britain, and resolves to meet again the following year.

1775 Parliament declares Massachusetts to be "in rebellion." After fighting breaks out, the Continental Congress sends a petition to George III appealing for peace; it is rejected.

America's first official flag

1775 As 1775 ends, Patriot naval officer John Paul Jones raises the first American flag authorized by the Continental Congress.

Carpenter's Hall

1774 Ann Lee, leader of the religious sect known as the Shakers, leaves Britain to found a religious community at Watervliet, New York.
• The British Parliament passes the Quebec Act, part of which guarantees French-Canadian Catholics freedom of worship; the act is opposed by many in the largely Protestant British colonies.

1775 Francis Salvador is elected to the South Carolina provincial congress. He is the first Jewish official elected in the colonies, and declares, "There is a time to pray and a time to fight."
• Lutheran pastor (and member of the Virginia Legislature) John Peter Muhlenberg urges colonists to support the Patriot cause. According to modern research, more than 3,000 church congregations or religious groups exist in the colonies at this time; in order according to numbers of members, they are Congregational, Presbyterian, Baptist, Anglican, Quaker, Dutch and German Reformed, Lutheran, and Roman Catholic. In addition, there are a number of smaller sects, including the Moravians, Mennonites, and Shakers, and about 2,500 Jews. The rapidly approaching conflict divides colonial churches.

Christ's Church, Philadelphia (founded by Anglicans in 1723)

UNDER BRITISH RULE

Before 1763, Britain was not deeply involved in the daily business of colonial governments. One reason for this was that many changes were taking place in English politics and society. In the Glorious Revolution of 1688, for example, the English Parliament removed the Catholic king James II from the throne and replaced him with Queen Mary and her husband, Prince William of Orange. William and Mary were Protestant rulers who were prepared to allow Parliament a greater role in governing.

Originally, many of the colonies were considered the personal property of the king. Now that royal power was limited, the task of governing the colonies fell to Parliament. But because Parliament had no central-ized, effective means of ruling all these different communities, it was easier to view the colonies as economic holdings rather than political ones. During this period, the systems of self-government that were already in place in the colonies became steadily more powerful. The settlers grew to consider self-government a basic right rather than a temporary situation that happened to be convenient for their British rulers.

Many people in Britain were critical of George III. They feared that his style of government would limit the authority of Parliament and threaten their own liberties as British citizens. This British cartoon (below) shows George sitting on a pedestal that proclaims his absolute power. The figure of the bound woman below him represents Britain. The artist depicts the idea that George's policies are tearing Britain apart with such vices as "ignorance" (stupidity), "venality" (corruption), "tyr-anny," and "despotism" (both expressions of harsh rule). The winged figure to the left represents Liberty, flying sadly away toward America.

George III (1738-1820; left) was crowned king after the death of his grandfather, King George II, in 1760. The new king wanted to strengthen the power of the monarchy and weaken the influence of his opponents in Parliament. He used the colonies to achieve this goal by promoting laws that restricted and taxed colonial trade, beginning with the Sugar Act in 1764.

GREAT IS OUR LORD, AND GREAT IS HIS POWER: YEA, AND HIS WISDOM IS INFINITE.

SELF-GOVERNMENT IN THE COLONIES

For their own survival in the wilderness, the earliest settlers created governments that maintained order, protected them from Indians and European enemies, and oversaw their towns' growth. At first, the colonists did not question the authority of the English crown, but they realized that they were better able to make decisions on local affairs than were their rulers across the Atlantic. The English government was not only far away, but was often inefficient. Overseers in England generally left local matters up to the colonists, while keeping the right to reject any decisions that threatened England's national interests.

In most cases, each colony had a governor and an assembly of legislators and advisers. Although the governor was usually appointed by the king, the council members were chosen from the community. By the second half of the 1700s, these patterns of governing were firmly in place. The colonists had grown so accustomed to their freedom that they were angry and resentful when Britain started trying to limit their power.

This woodcut (above) shows a colonial court of law. Citizens are gathered at a table discussing their complaints with a judge, seated in robes at the far right. The colonists prided themselves on the fairness of their system, which was available to rich and poor alike. The poem accompanying the illustration celebrates the power of the law to deliver justice:

How blest is that INTERPRETER OF LAWS
Who rich and Poor make equal in a Cause!
Who dares with steady hand the Balance hold,
And ne'er inclines it to one Side for Gold.

This courthouse (right) was built in Hanover, Virginia, in 1735. Many colonial judges, like the governor, were appointed by the king of England, but they were usually free to make decisions without royal interference. They worked with colonial juries to solve legal disputes. The colonial legal system grew out of English Common Law and was a basis for the legal system of the United States.

THE STAMP ACT CRISIS

Parliament passed two laws in the 1760s that reminded the colonies of Britain's power over them. Both laws, the Sugar Act and the Stamp Act, were intended to raise money to keep British soldiers in the colonies. The Sugar Act, passed in April 1764, was directed mainly at merchants. It placed taxes on imported sugar, rum, and molasses. The Stamp Act, on the other hand, applied to all citizens and had very little to do with trade. Passed by Parliament in 1765, the Stamp Act was a tax on such everyday consumer items as colonial newspapers, licenses, almanacs, and playing cards.

The Stamp Act brought forward the whole issue of taxation and government. The colonists felt that because they did not have their own representatives in Parliament they were being taxed without their consent. "No taxation without representation" became the rallying cry of the critics. To protest the Act, many colonists agreed not to buy any goods imported from Britain. Patrick Henry, one of the leaders of the protest, drafted the resolutions known as the Virginia Resolves, which stated that Parliament had no right to tax the colonists of Virginia. Meanwhile, in Boston, a group of objectors known as the Sons of Liberty began organizing protests against the acts.

The Stamp Act took effect on November 1, 1765. The day before, publisher William Bradford had put out the final edition of his newspaper, The Pennsylvania Journal and Weekly Advertiser, *which he "killed" because of the tax on newspapers. On the front page (opposite page, top), he adorned the masthead with a skull and crossbones, a gravedigger's tools, and a heavy black border in the shape of a tombstone.*

This engraving (opposite page, bottom) by Paul Revere shows a monument that the Sons of Liberty proposed building when the Stamp Act was repealed in March 1766. The figures at the top are portraits of various British officials, including King George III and William Pitt, who supported the colonists and helped bring about the repeal of the Act. The writing describes the outrage caused by the Stamp Act, and the gratitude and triumph the colonists felt when it was repealed.

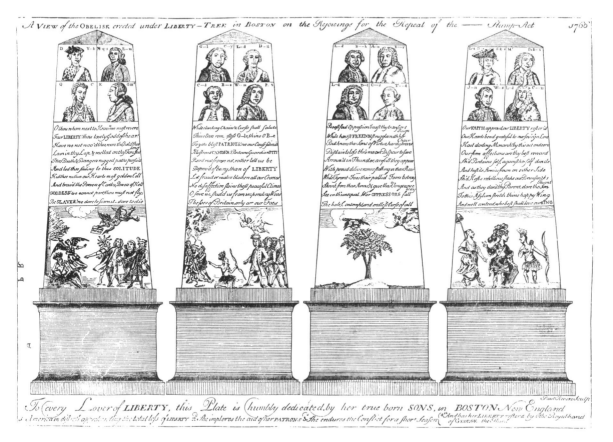

Some merchants, *afraid of losing money, cooperated with Britain. Merchants who were not sympathetic to the revolutionary cause were often singled out and mocked publicly. This issue of the* Boston Gazette *(above) lists merchants who continued to import British goods in spite of boycott agreements.*

The violence surrounding the Stamp Act protests in Boston convinced the British government to begin sending troops to restore order in the town. This print (below) by Paul Revere shows British transports arriving in Boston Harbor in 1768.

*In this German engraving from 1784 (above), a Boston mob
protests the Stamp Act by throwing stamped documents into a
bonfire. Riots and protests such as this one finally convinced
Parliament to repeal the Stamp Act after less than a year.*

THE STAMP ACT IS REPEALED

Parliament repealed the Stamp Act in March 1766, as a result of the violent protests and the boycotts which had harmed Britain's trade with the colonies. The colonists greeted the news with joy and immediately lifted boycotts on British goods. On the same day it repealed the Stamp Act, however, Parliament passed another measure that again outraged the colonists. The Declaratory Act stated that Parliament could pass any law it wished "to bind the colonies and people of America." Determined to maintain its power, Parliament imposed new taxes in the form of the Townshend Acts in June 1767. These Acts taxed glass, lead, paints, paper, and tea imported to the colonies. As with the Stamp Act, the colonists responded with a fresh boycott of British goods.

SUPPLEMENT to the PENNSYLVANIA JOURNAL, *EXTRAORDINARY.*

PHILADELPHIA, *May* 19, 1766.

This Morning arrived Capt. WISE, in a Brig from POOL in 8 Weeks, by whom we have the GLORIOUS NEWS of the

REPEAL OF THE STAMP-ACT,

As paſſed by the *King, Lords* and *Commons.* It received the ROYAL ASSENT the 18th of March, on which we moſt ſincerely congratulate our Readers.

An Act to repeal an Act made in the laſt Seſſion of Parliament, entituled, *An Act for granting and applying cert*ain *Stamp Duties, and other Duties, in the British Colonies and Plantations in America, towards further defraying the Expences of defending, protecting and ſecuring the ſame; and for amending ſuch Parts of the ſeveral Acts of Parliament, relating to the Trade and Revenues of the ſaid Colonies and Plantations, as direct the Manner of determining and recovering the Penalties and Forfeitures therein mentioned.*

H E R E A S an Act was paſſed in the laſt Parliament, intituled, *An Act for granting and applying certain Stamp Duties, in the British Colonies and Plantations in America, towards further defraying the expences of defending, protecting, and ſecuring the ſame; and for amending ſuch parts of the ſeveral Acts of Parliament relating to the Trade and Revenues of the ſaid Colonies and Plantations, as directed the Manner of determining and recovering the Penalties and Forfeitures therein mentioned:* And whereas the Continuance of the ſaid Act would be attended with many Inconveniencies, and may be productive of Conſequences greatly detrimental to the Commercial Intereſts of theſe Kingdoms; May it therefore pleaſe your moſt Excellent Majeſty, that it may be enacted; and be it enacted by the King's moſt Excellent Majeſty, by and with the Advice and Conſent of the Lords Spiritual and Temporal, and Commons, in this preſent Parliament aſſembled, and by the authority of the ſame, That from and after the Firſt Day of *May,* One thouſand ſeven hundred and ſixty ſix, the above-mentioned Act, and the ſeveral Matters and Things therein contained, ſhall be, and is and are hereby repealed and made void to all Intents and Purpoſes whatſoever.

With the help of the printing press, news of the repeal of the Stamp Act spread quickly through the colonies. This supplement to the Pennsylvania Journal *(above) describes the repeal in great detail. Because news from Britain traveled by ship, it took eight weeks for the colonists to learn of the repeal.*

THE REPEAL

OR THE FUNERAL OF MISS AME-STAMP

The Stamp Act was not entirely popular in Britain. Many Britons, especially merchants, were relieved when Parliament repealed the law. This British cartoon (above) shows George Grenville, the author of the Stamp Act (fourth from left), carrying his failed law in a child's coffin. The print became the most popular cartoon among Americans during the revolutionary era.

THE BOSTON MASSACRE

Colonial protests increased when Parliament refused to repeal the Townshend Acts. Protestors, who began to call themselves the Patriots, spoke out with their views on government and taxation, convincing more and more citizens to join their cause. The situation became a crisis when Lord Hillsborough, a British foreign minister, ordered the governor of Massachusetts to disband the colony's assembly. He also sent two regiments of British troops into Boston, a decision that led still more Americans to believe that Britain was determined to take away their liberties. Tensions ran high between the soldiers and the townspeople. On March 5, 1770, a fist fight broke out between a Boston worker and a British soldier. When a group of colonists joined the fight and began jeering at a guard outside the Old State House, the encounter quickly became a riot. The Redcoats fired into the angry crowd, killing five people. The tragedy caused such fear and outrage in the streets that to avoid a full-scale uprising, Parliament ordered all British troops to withdraw from the city.

Laſt Wedneſday Night died, *Patrick Carr*, an Inhabitant of this Town, of the Wound he received in King-Street on the bloody and execrable Night of the 5th Inſtant——He had juſt before left his Home, and upon his coming into the Street received the fatal Ball in his Hip which paſſed out at the oppoſite Side ; this is the fifth Life that has been ſacrificed by the Rage of the Soldiery, but it is feared it will not be the laſt, as ſeveral others are dangerouſly languiſhing of their Wounds. His Remains were attended on Saturday laſt from Faneuil-Hall by a numerous and reſpectable Train of Mourners, to the *ſame* Grave, in which thoſe who fell by the *ſame* Hands of Violence were interred the laſt Week.

These coffins (above and opposite page, bottom) appeared in a broadside published by Paul Revere. This printed announcement, which was posted and widely circulated, is an example of the kind of propaganda that used the Boston Massacre to rally more citizens to the Patriot cause. Each coffin bears the initials of one of the five victims, among them a black man named Crispus Attucks.

As anger toward Britain grew, Patriots realized that the colonies would have to stand together to challenge Parliament's authority. Benjamin Franklin's emblem for unity, the snake divided into parts that he drew in 1754 to promote the Albany Plan, appears once again on the front page of the Massachusetts Spy (opposite page, top), a Patriot newspaper.

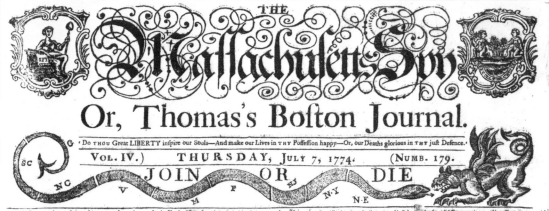

THE

Massachusetts Spy

Or, Thomas's Boston Journal.

'Do THOU Great LIBERTY inspire our Souls—And make our Lives in THY Poffeffion happy—Or, our Deaths glorious in THY juft Defence.'

VOL. IV.)   THURSDAY, JULY 7, 1774.   (NUMB. 179.

JOIN   OR   DIE

Hours to the Gates of this City many Thousands of our brave Brethren in the Country, deeply affected with our Diftreffes, and to whom we are greatly obliged on this Occafion—No one knows where this would have ended, and what important Confequences even to the whole British Empire might have followed, which our Moderation & Loyalty upon fo trying an Occafion, and our Faith in the Commander's Affurances have happily prevented.

Laft Thurfday, agreeable to a general Requeft of the Inhabitants, and by the Confent of Parents and Friends, were carried to their *Grave* in Succeffion, the Bodies of *Samuel Gray, Samuel Maverick, James Caldwell,* and *Crispus Attucks,* the unhappy Victims who fell in the bloody Maffacre of the Monday Evening preceding!

On this Occafion moft of the Shops in Town were fhut, all the Bells were ordered to toll a folemn Peal, as were alfo thofe in the neighboring Towns of Charleftown Roxbury, &c. The Proceffion began to move between the Hours of 4 and 5 in the Afternoon; two of the unfortunate Sufferers, viz. Meff. James Caldwell and Crispus

THE BURNING OF THE *GASPEE*

Determined to control widespread smuggling into the colonies, Britain sent customs ships to patrol the Atlantic coast. One of them, the *Gaspee*, was particularly forceful, stopping even small vessels and confiscating their goods. In June 1771, the *Gaspee* ran aground near Providence, Rhode Island. A colonist named John Smith, who had his own grievances against British tax collectors, led a band of men aboard the *Gaspee*. They shot and killed the captain, sent the crew ashore, and set the ship on fire. The culprits were caught and would have been sent for trial in England except that all witnesses refused to testify against them. The incident convinced many in Britain that the Americans were completely lawless and could not be brought to justice by fair, customary means.

Thomas Hutchinson (1711–80; above), the royal governor of Massachusetts, was a strong supporter of British rule. He disapproved of any moves on the part of the colonists that might undermine Parliament's authority. Immediately after the Gaspee *incident, Hutchinson announced that from then on he would receive his salary directly from the Crown instead of from the local legislature. This move took away one of the assembly's most significant powers.*

The Rhode Island colonists, led by John Smith, boarded the Gaspee *in the middle of the night and ordered the crew members to shore before setting the vessel on fire, as shown (right) in this nineteenth-century engraving.*

THE BOSTON TEA PARTY

The boycott of British goods in response to the Townshend Acts was a success. Three years later, in 1770, Parliament repealed all of the Acts but one, the tax on tea. When colonists began smuggling in cheaper tea from Holland, the British East India Company (which had a monopoly on the sale of British tea) lost money. In the spring of 1773, Parliament passed the Tea Act, which was designed to protect the East India Company from further losses. The Tea Act allowed the East India Company to sell its tea in the colonies at much lower prices. As a result, other tea merchants, unable to match these prices, were driven out of the colonial tea market. While some colonists were tempted to buy the East India Company's high-quality tea at very low prices, others resented the manner in which Parliament was using the Act to interfere with their marketplace. Protesting this latest outrage became a measure of patriotic honor. Tea ships were turned away from American ports, and many Americans refused to drink tea altogether while huge cargoes of it rotted in warehouses.

Tensions surrounding the Tea Act increased after the merchant ship Dartmouth arrived in Boston on November 27, 1773. Angry colonists, led by Samuel Adams, were determined to stop the ship from landing its cargo of tea. Governor Thomas Hutchinson was equally determined to collect the tax and enforce the law. On the night of December 16, a band of colonists disguised themselves as Indians and boarded the ship. While a crowd cheered them on from the wharf, they dumped all the chests of tea into Boston Harbor, as shown in this British print (above) from 1789.

ADVERTISEMENT.

THE Members of the Association of the Sons of Liberty, are requested to meet at the City-Hall, at one o'Clock, To-morrow, (being Friday) on Business of the utmost Importance;—And every other Friend to the Liberties, and Trade of America, are hereby most cordially invited, to meet at the same Time and Place. *The Committee of the Association.*

Thursday, NEW-YORK, 16th December, 1773.

This advertisement (above) announces a meeting of the Sons of Liberty, a Patriot organization that opposed Parliament's trade restrictions. The group, which had organized the Boston Tea Party, staged many riots and protests. The Sons of Liberty also printed handbills (pamphlets) that attacked the British government.

Protests against the Tea Act continued long after the Boston Tea Party. As news of the Boston Tea Party spread throughout the colonies, other communities joined the protest. This British engraving from 1775 (left) shows a "Society of Patriotic Ladies" from North Carolina meeting to draw up a pledge to drink no more tea. While some are signing the pledge, others are emptying their tea containers.

One of the most outspoken critics of British trade restrictions was Samuel Adams (1722-1803; right), who launched protests against both the Stamp Act and the Townshend Acts in the 1760s. His stirring articles and speeches increased anti-British feeling. A founder of the Sons of Liberty, Adams was an important player in the events that led up to the Boston Tea Party. When the Dartmouth came into Boston Harbor, it was Adams who, with his speeches and slogans, provoked the crowds to prevent the cargo from coming ashore. Samuel Adams was first cousin to John Adams, one of the signers of the Declaration of Independence in 1776 and later the second President of the United States.

THE INTOLERABLE ACTS

In the spring of 1774, Parliament responded to the Boston Tea Party by passing the Coercive Acts, which became known as the "Intolerable Acts." The first of these harsh new laws, the Boston Port Act, closed the harbor of Boston to all ships until its citizens paid for the wasted tea. The Massachusetts Government Act changed the original charter for the colony of Massachusetts drastically, giving more power to the governor while weakening the authority of local town councils. Council members were now appointed by the royal governor instead of elected by the people. The Intolerable Acts, which punished an entire population for the crimes committed by a few individuals, outraged the colonists. Patriotic feeling spread through the colonies as more and more citizens refused to respect British authority. Other communities showed their support for the people of Massachusetts, aware now that Parliament could rule them just as harshly if it chose to. The Virginia House of Burgesses declared a day of fasting to show sympathy for the citizens of Boston, who were facing food shortages now that their port was closed. South Carolina shipped money and rice to the city, while New York sent sheep.

This cartoon (above), entitled "The Patriotick Barber of New York, or the Captain in the Suds," shows a barber throwing a British soldier out of his shop to demonstrate his support for the Patriot cause. When the cartoon was published in New York in October 1774, it appeared beside this declaration: "It is most devoutly to be wished that all Gentlemen of the Razor will follow this wise, prudent, interesting and praiseworthy example."

The rebel colonists could be ruthless when harassing and punishing representatives of British authority. In this illustration (above), an angry mob prepares to cover a customs official with tar and feathers. He is being lowered into a wagon, in which he will be paraded through the streets of Boston to complete his humiliation.

CARTOONS AND PUBLIC SENTIMENT IN BRITAIN

As relations between Britain and the colonies grew tense, Patriots did whatever they could to increase anti-British feeling. Posters, advertisements, and broadsides all condemned Parliament's acts as hateful and tyrannical. The passage of the Intolerable Acts in the spring of 1774 heightened the struggle. The British public began taking a greater interest in the political situation in the colonies. Many British citizens supported the Patriots' cause, which seemed to them a struggle for the freedoms and privileges due any British subject. They were disturbed to see Parliament punishing the colonies by imposing taxes and trade restrictions. It seemed that Parliament was behaving like an autocratic ruler toward the colonies, when only a century earlier, in the Glorious Revolution, Parliament had triumphed over a monarchy to defend the rights of the people. Many Britons, particularly merchants and shipowners, suffered business losses. They urged Parliament to cooperate with the colonies in order to restore healthy trade with America. British supporters made their views known by publishing cartoons, many of which openly criticized the government.

While many prominent British citizens took an interest in American political affairs, they did not always support or respect the colonist's arguments. This British cartoon from about 1775 (above) makes fun of two British politicians in a bathroom (known in colonial times as a "privy" or "necessary house"). They are showing a casual interest in political pamphlets written by the colonists. The man on the right is wiping his hands on a paper listing the resolutions of the Continental Congress, while the other sits reading a book entitled Answer to a P[amphlet En]titled Taxation [No] Tir[anny].

This British cartoon (right), called "A Political Lesson," was published in September 1774. It shows Thomas Gage, the newly-appointed governor of Massachusetts, being thrown from his horse. (The horse represents the rebellious colonies.) In the summer of 1774, Gage had attempted to end popular unrest by moving the government from Boston to Salem and dissolving the assembly. His plan met with stubborn refusals, and in August he was forced to return the government to Boston.

THE FIRST CONTINENTAL CONGRESS

In 1774, the colonies realized that the best way to approach Britain with their complaints was through a unified governmental body. Many Patriots feared that protests, riots, and other acts would only encourage Parliament to impose greater restrictions and taxes. On September 5, the first Continental Congress, made up of delegates from twelve of the colonies, met in Philadelphia. The purpose of the meeting was to find ways to restore good relations between the colonies and Britain. When the Congress's first session ended on October 26, the delegates had accomplished several things. They first drafted a statement to King George III that declared the rights of the colonies and listed their grievances. They also formed the Continental Association to organize a formal boycott of British goods. This move was different from previous boycotts because it also proposed to ban American exports to Britain. The colonists hoped this plan would bring pressure on Parliament to relax its trade restrictions. The delegates also agreed to meet again in Philadelphia on May 10, 1775.

Thomas Jefferson (1743–1826; above) was a member of the Virginia House of Burgesses at the time of the First Continental Congress. He wrote a pamphlet entitled A Summary View of the Rights of British America, *which was intended as instructions for the Virginia delegates. Widely read when it appeared in August 1774, the pamphlet argued that Parliament had no authority over the colonies and that allegiance to the king should be voluntary.*

At first, the Continental Congress was to meet in the Pennsylvania Statehouse, but the delegates chose instead to meet in Carpenters' Hall. The move was considered "highly agreeable to the mechanics and citizens in general," and symbolized the democratic nature of the Congress. This engraving (right), which appeared in a French book in 1782, shows the Congress's first session.

John Adams (1735-1826; left) was a lawyer from Boston who attended the first meeting of the Continental Congress as a Massachusetts delegate, along with Samuel Adams, his cousin. John Adams first became involved in politics as a strong opponent of the Stamp Act. He spoke eloquently for colonial rights during the first meeting and went on to attend the Second Continental Congress in 1775.

This sketch shows Patrick Henry (1736-99) addressing an assembly of colonial leaders (above). A member of the Virginia House of Burgesses, Henry was instrumental in organizing the First Continental Congress in 1774. He was a distinguished orator (public speaker) and politician. The following year he urged his fellow Virginians to take up arms to defend their rights, saying: "I know not what course others may take, but as for me, give me liberty or give me death."

Shown here (opposite page, bottom) are the first and last pages of the First Continental Congress's petition to George III. Among their grievances the delegates listed the British standing army, the taxes on colonial trade, and the changes to colonial charters. Following the list of grievances is a declaration of the rights of the colonies. The last page shows the signatures of the delegates; all colonies except Georgia were represented in this petition.

EPILOGUE: THE CONSTITUTIONAL CONVENTION

The Americans won their independence from Britain in October 1781, when Lord Charles Cornwallis surrendered his forces at Yorktown, thus ending the Revolutionary War. In the mid-1780s, it was clear to many American leaders that a stronger, more centralized form of government than that provided by the Articles of Confederation was necessary for the young nation's survival. A convention was organized in Philadelphia in the summer of 1787. Fifty-five delegates, representing all the states except Rhode Island, attended to debate which form the national government should take.

The "Virginia Plan" proposed that the number of representatives from each state would be determined by the size of its population, thereby favoring states with large populations. The "New Jersey Plan" proposed giving all states an equal number of representatives. The solution came with the "Connecticut Compromise," which established the two houses of Congress: The Senate would have two members from each state, while the House of Representatives would represent each state according to the size of its population. The Constitution was officially adopted on June 21, 1788, after nine out of the thirteen states had ratified it.

James Madison (1751-1836; above) was the author of the Virginia Plan, which proposed allotting each state its representatives according to the size of its population. To promote ratification of the Constitution, Madison wrote a series of essays, along with John Jay and Alexander Hamilton, which became known as The Federalist Papers.

The United States Constitution (opposite page, top) is the oldest national charter in the world that is still in effect. One of its most important features is its provision for separating power between three separate branches of government: the legislative, the judicial, and the executive. The balance between these three parts was designed to prevent any one branch from seizing power from the others.

This cartoon (opposite page, bottom) comments on the turmoil among the states just before the Constitutional Convention convened. The cart, stuck in mud, represents the state of the new nation's government in 1787. The authors of the Constitution were charged with the duty of saving the states from chaos and forming an effective government to direct them in the future.

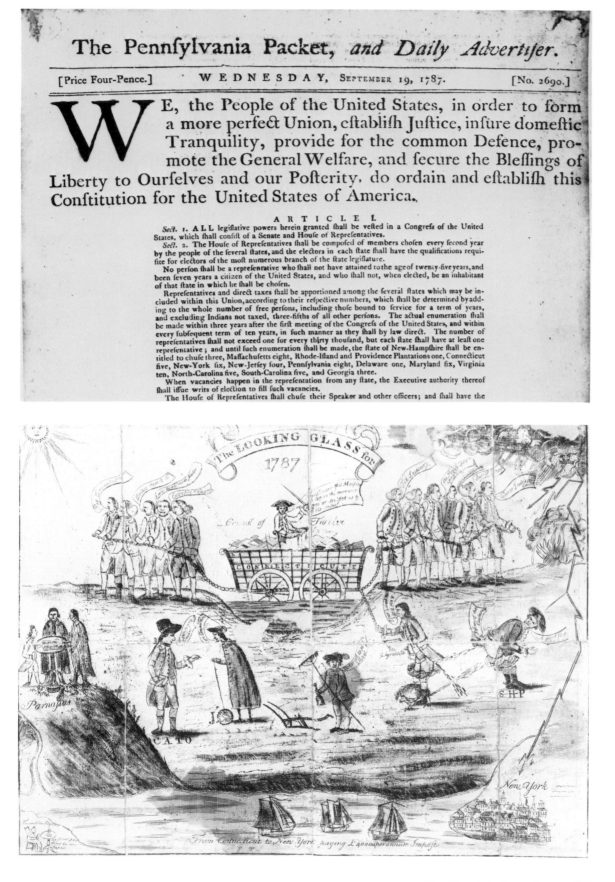

Resource Guide

Key to picture positions: (T) top, (C) center, (B) bottom; and in combinations: (TL) top left, (TC) top center, (TR) top right, (BL) bottom left, (BC) bottom center, (BR) bottom right, (CR) center right, (CL) center left.

Key to picture locations within the Library of Congress collections (and where available, photo negative numbers): P - Prints and Photographs; HABS - Historical American Buildings Survey (div. of Prints and Photographs); R - Rare Book Division; G - General Collections; MSS - Manuscript Division; G&M - Geography and Map Division.

PICTURES IN THIS VOLUME

2-3 Philadelphia, P, USZ62-3282 6-7 Brewster, P, USZ62-12707 8-9 Map, G 10-11 Capitol, P, SZ62-2104

Timeline I:
12 T, Columbus, P, USZ62-4408; C, Pope, P, USZ62-49700; BL, Las Casas, P; BR, Coronado, P, USZ62-37993 13 T, mercenary, G; CL, totem, G; CR, Seal, G; BL, Jesuit, R; BR, ruins, G 14 TL, Mayflower, R; TC, Charles I, R; TR, Adolphus, G; B, Williams, G 15 TL, Montreal, R; TR, Cromwell, R; CL, Opechancanough, P, USZ62-8962; CR, Stuyvesant, P, USZ62-1837 16-17 C, Columbus, P, USZ62-4408; BR, landing, P, USZ62-5970 18-19 TL, Las Casas, P; BL, Jesuits, R; TR, Indians, P, USZ62-49750 20-21 TR, Laudonnière, P, USZ62-374; BR, map, P, USZ62-381 22-23 TL, Raleigh, P, USZ62-2951; TR, chief, P, USZ62-89909; BR, chief's wife, P, USZ62-76084. 24-25 TL, Smith, P, USZ62-10751; TR, Indians, P 26-27 TR, map, G&M; BR, Mayflower, P, USZ62-8280 28-29 TL, Winthrop, P, USZ62-1004; TR, title page, R; BR, villagers, R 30-31 TL, title page, R; TR, Harvard, P, USZ62-45523; BR, Cotton, P, USZ62-96226 32-33 Whitefield, P, USZ62-45506

Timeline II:
34 T, fire, G; B, Quakers, G 35 T, Louis XIV, G;C, Locke, G; B, meeting house, P, HABS-Mass.-12- 36 TL, Marlborough, G; TR, Seal, P, USZ62-676; C, cottage, P,USZ62-33765 37 TL, Frederick II, G; TC, Maria Theresa, G; TR, Colloden, G; C, cartoon, P, USZ62-9701; BL, college, G; BR, Edwards, P, USZ62-21212 38-39 TL, Moravians, P, USZ62-41998; TR, Quakers, P, USZ62-5808 40-41 TL, Penn, P, USZ62-12218; TR, title page, R; BR, house, R 42-43 TL, Andros, P, USZ62-30882; TR, Stuyvesant, P 44-45 TL, title page, R; TR, Eliot, P, USZ62-3025; BR, missionaries, R 46-47 TR, meeting house, P, HABS; BR, trial, P, USZ62-475 48-49 TR, title page, P, USZ62-58190; BR, Yale, P, USZ62-02102 50-51 TL, Geography, R; TR, title page, R; BR, Library, P, HABS

52-53 TR, Edwards, P, USZ62-21212; BR, orphanage, P, USZ62-51640 54-55 BL, church, P, USZ62-46025; TR, synagogue, P, HABS 56-57 TL, Lappawinsoe, G; TR, ceremony, P, USZ62-34019 58-59 TR, map, R; BR, cartoon, P, USZ62-9701 60-61 Massacre, P, USZ62-11221.

Timeline III:
62 T, Catherine, G; C, Braddock, P, USZ62-51691; BL, seminary, G; BR, synagogue, P, HABS RI-Newp. 29-1 63 T, Cook, G; B, Serra, G 64 TL, North, G; TC, Parliament, P, USZ62-1-79; TR, George III, P, USZ62-21623; CL, coffins, P, USZ62-45586; CR, Patriots, P, USZ62-48562; BL, Jefferson, G; BR, interior, P, HABS RI-3-Newp.29-9 65 TL, steam engine, G; TR, Burke, G; CL, Carpenter's Hall, P, USZ62-2797; CR, flag, G; B, church, P, USZ62-46025 66-67 TR, George III, P, USZ62-15553; BR, cartoon, P, USZ62-45443 68-69 TR, court, P, USZ62-45567; BR, court house, P, HABS, s35-RP 26-1 70-71 TR, Journal, P, USZ62-21637, BR, cartoon, P, USZ62-22385 72-73 TL, Gazette, P, USZ62-45585; BL, troops, P, USZ62-45559; TR, protest, P, USZ61-449 74-75 TL, Repeal, P; TR, cartoon, P, USZ62-21264 76-77 TL, coffin, P, USZ62-45587; TR, title page, P, USZ62-7984; BR, coffins, P, USZ62-45586 78-79 TL, Hutchinson, P, USZ62-25249; TR, Gaspee; P, USZ62-15926 80-81 Ship, P, USZ62-48562 82-83 TL, advertisement, MSS; TR, Ladies; P, USZ62-12711; BR, Adams, P, USZ62-46607 84-85 TL, Barber, P, USZ62-17658; TR, cartoon, P, USZ62-39581 86-87 TL, cartoon, P, USZ62-1511; TR, horse, P, USZ62-22038 88-89 TL, Jefferson, P, USZ62-7583; TR, Adams, P, USZ62-45280; BR, Congress, P, USZ62-45328 90-91 TR, Henry, P, USZ62-51569; BR, petition, MSS 92-93 TL, Madison, P, USZ62-36775; TR, title page, P, USZ62-58266; BR, cartoon, P, USZ62-96402.

SUGGESTED READING

FISHER, DOROTHY CANFIELD. *Our Independence and the Constitution.* New York: Random House, 1987.

MCPHILLIPS, MARTIN. *The Constitutional Convention.* Englewood Cliffs, NJ: Silver Burdett, 1986.

PAINE, THOMAS AND THOMAS JEFFERSON. *Paine and Jefferson on Liberty.* New York: Ungar, 1988.

SHENKMAN, RICHARD. *Legends, Lies, and Cherished Myths of American History.* New York: William Morrow, 1988.

SMITH, CARTER. *The Jamestown Colony.* New York: Silver Burdett, 1991.

ENCYCLOPEDIA BRITTANICA. *The Annals of America, volumes 1, 2, 3.* Chicago: Encyclopedia Brittanica, Inc. 1976.

The American Heritage Illustrated History of the United States, volumes 1, 2, 3, and 4. New York: American Heritage, 1988.

The Life History of the United States, volumes 1, 2, and 3. Alexandria, Virginia, 1977.

Index

Page numbers in *italics* indicate illustrations.

Act of Union, 66
Adams, John, 83, *89*
Adams, Samuel, 81, *83, 89*
Albany Plan, 58, 59, 76
almanacs, *49*
Amadas, Philip, 22
Andros, Edmund, *42*
Anglican Church, *54*
Athore, 20, *21*
Attucks, Crispus, 76
Avilés, Pedro Menéndez de, 20

Barlowe, Arthur, 22
Bay Psalm Book, *30*
Bethlehem, Pennsylvania, 38
Bible, in Indian language, *44*
Bill of Rights, 92
books
  about Indian language, *29*
  almanacs, *49*
  Bay Psalm Book, *30*
  for children, 50, *51*
  Indian bible, *44*
  in libraries, 50, *51*
  textbooks, 50
Boston, Massachusetts
  Massacre, *60*, 61, 76
  port closing in, 84
  Stamp Act protests, 70, 72, *73*
  Tea Party, *80-81*, 80, 83, 84
Boston Port Act, 84
Bradford, William, 26, *27*, 70
Brewster, William, *6*
Britain. *See* England
broadsides, 61, *76*, 86
Bry, Theodore de, *17, 19*

calumet ceremony, 56, 57
Carpenter's Hall, *89*
cartoons, *59*, 61, *66-67*, 84, *86, 87*
Cayuga Indians, 58
Charles I, King, 28, 33
children
  books for, 50, *51*
  in schools, 48, *50*
Coercive Acts, 84
colleges, 11, *16-17*, 31, *48-49*, 52
Columbus, Christopher, 11, 16, *16-17*
Common Law, 68
Congress, 92
Connecticut, 9, 48
Connecticut Compromise, 92
Conquistadores, 18, 19
Constitution, 92, *93*
Constitutional Convention, 92, *93*
Continental Association, 88

Continental Congress, First, 88, *89*, 90, *91*
Cornwallis, Charles, 92
Cotton, John, *31*
courts, 68, *69*
  witchcraft trials, 46, *47*
Cromwell, Oliver, 33

Dartmouth College, 52
Davidson, Robert, 50
Daye, Stephen, 30
Declaratory Act, 74
Delaware, 9, 40
Delaware Indians, 40, *56*
Dominion of New England, 42
Drake, Francis, 22

East India Company, 80
education, 30, *31*, 48
  See also books; colleges
Edwards, Jonathan, 33, 52, 53
Eliot, John, 44, *45*
Elizabeth I, Queen, 22
England
  Act of Union, 66
  in Boston Massacre, 76
  colonial expansion of, 33
  colonial settlements of, 9, 11, 22, 24, 26, 28
  criticism of George III in, *67*, 67
  French and Indian War, 61
  in *Gaspee* incident, 78, *79*
  Glorious Revolution, 66, 86
  Intolerable Act protests against, *84-85*, 84
  Puritans in, 33
  Quaker movement in, 38
  Stamp Act protests against, 70, *71, 72, 73*, 75
  support for Patriot cause in, 86
  surrender at Yorktown, 92
  takeover of New Amsterdam, 42, *43*
  tax policy of, 61, 66, 67, 70, 74, 75
  Tea Act protests against, *80-81*, 80, 83
  trade boycott against, 70, 72, 74, 80, 88
  trade restrictions of, 33, 61, 66, 80, 82, 83, 88
explorers
  Columbus, 11, *16-17*, 16
  conquistadores, 18
  English, 22

Federalist Papers, 92
Ferdinand, King, 16, *17*
Florida, Huguenots in, 20, *21*
Fort Caroline, 20
France
  French and Indian War, 61
  Huguenots, 20, *21*
  New France, 9, *45*
Franklin, Benjamin, 48, *49*, 58, 59, 76
French and Indian War, 61

Gage, Thomas, 86, *87*
Gaspee incident, 78, *79*
George II, King, 58
George III, King, 66, *67*, 70, 88, 90, *91*
Georgia, 9, 52
Glorious Revolution, 66, 86
government
  Albany Plan, 58, 59, 76
  in Constitution, 92
  Intolerable Acts and, 84
  Mayflower Compact, 26, *27*
  in New Amsterdam, 42
  in Pennsylvania, 40
  royal governors, 42, 68, 78, 84
  self-government, 33, 61, 66, 68, *69*
  and taxation issue, 70
  in Virginia, *10*, 11, 84, 90
Great Awakening, 33, 52, 53
Grenville, George, 75

Hamilton, Alexander, 92
Harvard, College, *31*
Harvard, John, 30
Henry, Patrick, 70, *90-91*, 90
Hesselius, Gustavus, 56
Hillsborough, Lord, 76
Hispaniola, 16, 19
Huguenots, 20
Hutchinson, Thomas, *78*, 78, 81

Indians
  calumet ceremony, 56, *57*
  conversion of, 11, 18, *19*, 44, *45*
  in Florida, 20
  French and Indian War, 61
  Iroquois Confederacy, *58-59*, 58
  language, 24, 29, 44
  religion, *21, 25*
  in Rhode Island, 29
  and Spanish, *17*, 19
  treaties with, 40, 56
  in Virginia, 22, 23, 24, *25*
Intolerable Acts, 84

Iroquois Confederacy, *58-59*, 58
Isabella, Queen, 16, *17*

James I, King, 24, 28
James II, King, 66
Jamestown colony, 9, 11, 24
Jay, John, 92
Jefferson, Thomas, 88
Jesuits, *18*, 19, 44, *45*
Jews, 54, 55

King's College, 52

Lappawinsoe, Chief, *56*
Las Casas, Bartolomé de, *18*, 19
Laudonnière, René de, 20
libraries, 50, *51*

Madison, James, *92*
Maryland, 9
Mary, Queen, 66
Massachusetts
    Andros's overthrow in, 42
    Dominion of New England, 42
    Intolerable Acts in, 84
    See also Boston, Massachu-
        setts; Puritans
Massachusetts Bay Colony, 9,
    28, 42, 48, 54
Massachusetts Government Act,
    84
Mather, Cotton, 46
Mayflower, 6, 26
Mayflower Compact, 26, *27*
meeting house, *10*, 11, 46, *47*
missionaries, *19*, 44, *45*
Mohawk Indians, 58
Moravians, *38*
Morgues, Jacques Le Moyne de,
    20

Narragansett Indians, 29
New Amsterdam, 9, 42, *43*
New France, 9, 45
New Hampshire, 9
New Jersey, 9, 40
New Jersey Plan, 92
Newport, Rhode Island, 50, *51*,
    54, *55*
newspapers
    cartoons, *59*, 61, *66-67*,
        84, *86*, *87*
    Patriot, 76, *77*
    Stamp Act protests in, *71*, *72*
    tax on, 70
New York, 9, 84
    See also New Amsterdam
North Carolina, 9, 20, 22

Oneida Indians, 58
Onondaga Indians, 58
Opechancanough, *18*, 19

Patriots
    in Boston Massacre, 76
    British supporters of, 86
    newspaper of, 76, *77*
    propaganda of, 61, 76, 86
    Sons of Liberty, 70, 72,
        81, 82, 83
peace pipe ceremony, 56, *57*
Pennsylvania
    founding of, 9, 38, 40, *41*

Indian treaties, 40, 56
Moravians in, 38
Quakers in, 38, 40
religious freedom in, 40,
    54
    See also Philadelphia,
        Pennsylvania
Penn, Thomas, 56
Penn, William, 9, 38, *40*, *41*
Philadelphia, Pennsylvania, 40,
    41, *54*, 88, *89*, *92*
Phips, William, 46
Pilgrims, *6*, 9, 26, *27*
Pitt, William, 70
Plymouth Colony, 6, 26, *27*
Pocahontas, 24
Poor Richard's Almanac, *49*
Port Royal, 20
Princeton College, 52
Protestant Reformation, 11
Providence, Rhode Island, 29
Puritans
    and Indians, 44, *45*
    and education, 30, *31*, 48
    Massachusetts Bay Colony,
        9, 28, 42, 48, 54
    religion, 28, *29*, *30*, *31*,
        46, 47
    religious intolerance of,
        28, 33, 38, 54
    witchcraft trials of, 46, *47*

Quakers, 38, *39*, 42

Raleigh, Walter, *22*
Redwood Library, 50, 51
religion
    Anglican Church, *54*
    conversion of Indians, 11,
        18, *19*, 44, *45*
    freedom of, 11, 40, 54
    Great Awakening, 33, 52, 53
    Huguenots, 20, *21*
    Indian, *21*, *25*
    Jewish, 54, *55*
    Moravians, *38*
    of Pilgrims, 6, 26
    Protestant Reformation, 11
    Puritans, 28, *29*, *30*, *31*,
        46, 47
    Quakers, 38, *39*, 42
Revere, Paul, 61, 70, 72, 76
Rhode Island, 9, 92
    founding of, 28, 29, 54
    Gaspee incident in, 78, *79*
    Jews in, 54, 55
    See also Newport, Rhode
        Island
Ribaut, Jean, 20, *21*
Roanoke colony, 22
Roman Catholic Church, 9
    conversion of Indians, 11,
        18, *19*, 44, *45*

Salem, Massachusetts,
    witchcraft trials in,
    46, *47*
Seneca Indians, 58
Smith, John, *24*, 78, *79*
Sons of Liberty, 70, 72, 81,
    82, 83
South Carolina, 9, 84
Spain
    conquest of New World, 11,
        16-17, 16
    conquistadores, 18, 19

Florida settlement, 20
Hispaniola, 16, 19
Stamp Act
    protests against, 70-73,
        71, *72*, *73*
    repeal of, 70, *74* *75*
    taxes under, 70
    unpopularity in England, *75*
Stuyvesant, Peter, 42, *43*
Sugar Act, 66, 70
synagogue, 54, 55

taxation
    parliamentary policy of, 61
    Stamp Act, 70
    Sugar Act, 66, 70
    Townshend Acts, 74, 75, 80
    Tea Act, *80-81*, *80*, 83
Touro, Isaac, 54
Touro Synagogue, 54, 55
Townshend Acts, 74, 75, 80
trade
    boycott on British goods,
        70, 72, 74, 80, 88
    restrictions on, 33, 61,
        66, 80, 82, 83, 88
    taxes on, 70, 74
treaties, Indian, 40, 56
Treaty of Paris, 61
Tuscarora Indians, 58

Velasco, Don Luis de, *18*, 19
Virginia
    and Continental Congress, 8
    House of Burgesses, *10*, 11,
        84, 90
    Jamestown, 9, 11, 24, *25*
    Roanoke, 22
Virginia Company, 11, 24, 26
Virginia Plan, 92
Virginia Resolves, 70

Walking Purchase agreement, 56
Wesley, John, 52
Whitefield, George, *32*, 33, 52
White, John, 22, *25*
Whole Book of Psalms, The
    (Bay Psalm Book), 30
William of Orange, 66
Williamsburg, Virginia, 10
Williams, Roger, 28, 29, 54
Winthrop, John, 28
witchcraft trials, 46, *47*

Yale College, *48-49*, 48
Yale, Elihu, 48

Zinzendorf, Count, 38